Georgia

OFF THE BEATEN PATH™

"A rare, exceptional guidebook . . . facts and points of interest that the state promotional agency and local chamber of commerce had somehow overlooked . . . highly recommended for anyone who detests fast food restaurants and overpriced hotels and tourist attractions."
—*The Pike County (PA) Courier*

"Schemmel's guide will relay to you some of the more unusual and oft-not included sights available in the state."
—*Chattanooga News-Free Press*

"A dandy resource."
—*Atlanta Journal-Constitution*

"Delightful . . . William Schemmel's carefully researched book takes you up, down, and around the state of Georgia. . . . This guide is the perfect traveling companion."
—*Camp-orama*

Georgia

OFF <u>THE</u>

BEATEN

PATH™

THIRD EDITION

WILLIAM SCHEMMEL

A Voyager Book

The Globe Pequot Press

Old Saybrook, Connecticut

Cover map © DeLorme Mapping
Illustrations by Carole Drong

Library of Congress Cataloging-in-Publication Data
Schemmel, William.
    Georgia : off the beaten path / William Schemmel. — 3rd ed.
      p. cm. — (Off the beaten path series)
    "A Voyager book."
    Includes index.
    ISBN 1-56440-883-3
    1. Georgia—Guidebooks. I. Title. II. Series.
F284.3.S34   1996
917.5804'43—dc20   96-5070
                                                              CIP

Manufactured in the United States of America
Third Edition/Second Printing

To Richard Magruder,
Your wisdom and wit are greatly missed.

GEORGIA

Northwest

Northeast

Metro
Atlanta

Middle

Southeast

Coastal

Southwest

CONTENTS

INTRODUCTION

After spending a good deal of my life wandering Georgia's byways, I'm happily convinced it will never run out of ways to surprise and delight me. From the Blue Ridge Mountains by the Tennessee and Carolina borders to the Okefenokee Swamp and piny woods bordering Florida, from Savannah and "The Golden Isles" on the Atlantic Coast to Columbus and La Grange and Lake Seminole on the westerly Chattahoochee River, I'm ever amazed at my home state's depth and breadth. It's like an incredible attic stacked floor to ceiling with a never-ending cache of treasures.

I've attended Sunday morning services with Macon County's Mennonites and been transported by the Gregorian chants of the Benedictine monks at Rockdale County's Monastery of the Holy Ghost. I've awakened in the depths of the swamps to the eerie symphony of gators and owls and at sunrise by mountain lakes to the siren songs of loons and geese.

I've encountered ghosts, and tales of ghosts, in antebellum mansions where Sherman and Lafayette once slept, and I've half-believed the outrageous lies of fishermen and small-town sages. I've attended festivals exalting rattlesnakes, chitterlings, sorghum syrup, pecans, autumn leaves, spring dogwoods, and Greek, Chinese, Middle Eastern, East Indian, and American Indian heritage. Along the way I've eaten a fair share of barbecue, catfish, and fried chicken, as well as accomplished European cuisine, in mountain valleys and small-town cafes.

I've beheld a likeness of the Roman she-wolf nursing Romulus and Remus, donated to an embarrassed small town by Benito Mussolini, and best of all, I've met Georgia's proudest monument, her own people, in their natural habitat. A few grouches notwithstanding, they're warm, wise, witty, and when you wander off the beaten path, they'll be tickled to point you in some fascinating directions. With the Summer Olympic Games coming to Atlanta and Savannah in 1996, 6.5 million Georgians are ready to welcome unprecedented numbers of visitors.

I hope you'll enjoy using this book half as much as I've enjoyed researching it. When you discover some off-the-beaten-path adventures that I've yet to come across, please let me know by writing to me c/o The Globe Pequot Press, P.O. Box 833, Old Saybrook, CT 06475.

Restaurant cost categories refer to the price of entrees without beverages, desserts, taxes, or tips. Those listed as inexpensive are

$10 or less; moderate, between $10 and $15; and expensive $20 and over.

The prices and rates listed in this guidebook were accurate at press time, but I recommend that you call establishments before traveling in order to obtain current information.

In July and August 1996, Georgia welcomes the Centennial Summer Olympic Games. Most events will be held in the Atlanta metro area, but you may also catch some of the action in Columbus, Savannah, and Athens and in neighboring Alabama and Tennessee. If you're coming for the games, or any other time, communities throughout the state and region invite you to enjoy their attractions and hospitality.

Before you launch your Off the Beaten Path adventures, gather information from these sources: Georgia Tourist Division, P.O. Box 1776, Atlanta 30301, (404) 656–3590; and Georgia Department of Natural Resources, Parks and Historic Sites Division, 205 Butler Street, Suite 1352, Atlanta 30334. For general information call (800) 869–8420 from anywhere in the United States; in metro Atlanta call (404) 656–3530.

The Parks Division's new Reservation Resource lets you make one toll-free call for campsites, cottages, picnic shelters, and lodge rooms throughout the system. Rates vary at different parks. Campsites, with electrical and water hookups, range from $12 to $17 a night. Completely furnished cottages are $45 to $55 for one bedroom, $65 to $75 for two bedrooms, and $75 to $125 for three bedrooms. Rates are higher on weekends and in certain seasons. Double rooms at state park lodges are $48 to $70. In metro Atlanta call (770) 389–PARK; anywhere else in the United States call (800) 864–PARK.

If you're interested in a particular area, contact the local convention and visitors bureau or chamber of commerce.

METRO ATLANTA

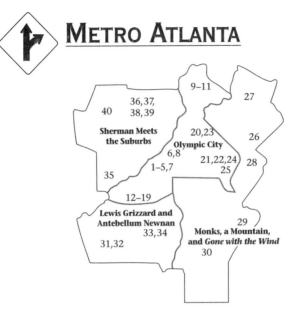

1. Welcome South Visitors Center
2. SCITREK Museum
3. Ansley Park
4. Atlanta Botanical Garden
5. Piedmont Park
6. Atlanta History Center
7. Zoo Atlanta
8. Georgia Governors Mansion
9. Chattahoochee River National Recreation Area
10. Chattahoochee Nature Center
11. Roswell
12. Atlanta Preservation Center
13. Oakland Cemetery
14. Wren's Nest
15. Center for Puppetry Arts
16. Herndon House
17. APEX Museum
18. Martin Luther King Jr. National Historic Site
19. Little Five Points
20. De Kalb County's "Little Asia"
21. Michael C. Carlos Emory University Museum of Art and Archaeology
22. Stone Mountain Village
23. Chamblee
24. The Atlanta Dream Hostel
25. Fernbank Museum of Natural History/Fernbank Science Center
26. Yellow River Wildlife Game Ranch
27. Sugar Hill Municipal Golf Course
28. Monastery of the Holy Ghost
29. Panola Mountain State Conservation Park
30. Cherokee Rose Shooting Resort
31. Antebellum Newnan Driving Tour of Homes
32. Lewis Grizzard/Erskine Caldwell Museums
33. The Buggy Shop Museum
34. Starr's Mill
35. Sweetwater Creek Conservation Park
36. Kennesaw Mountain National Battlefield Park
37. Big Shanty Museum
38. Marietta Town Square
39. Rocky Pine Ranch
40. Pickett's Mill Battlefield

METRO ATLANTA

OLYMPIC CITY

Before you begin exploring Atlanta, get your bearings at the ◆ **Welcome South Visitors Center** (404–224–2000). Downtown at Spring Street and International Boulevard, Welcome South is a walk-through attraction with high-tech audiovisuals, films, displays, a book and gift shop, and free information about Atlanta, other Georgia destinations, and neighboring states. Open daily.

Your first tour stop could be the ◆ **SCITREK Science and Technology Museum** (404–522–5500). Downtown at 395 Piedmont Avenue, the museum has dozens of hands-on gadgets that inquisitive kids and adults can push, pull, stand on, revolve around, and climb into. Open daily. Adults are $7.50; ages 3–17, seniors, and students with ID, $5.00.

Atlanta's first-time visitors are usually flabbergasted by the city's greenness. Thanks to a relatively high altitude—1,050 feet in the foothills of the Blue Ridge Mountains—and about fifty inches of rainfall, the city seems to swim in a sea of towering pines, hardwoods, magnolias, dogwoods, and azaleas. Residential neighborhoods and parks are especially blessed with trees, gardens, and flowers.

◆ **Ansley Park,** a lovely neighborhood dating back to the 1920s, is a soothing place to walk, drive, or ride a bike. On Peachtree Street at the Woodruff Arts Center/Colony Square area, turn east onto 15th Street, then left (north) onto Peachtree Circle, and follow the meandering byways past sumptuous lawns and gardens skirting homes in a spectrum of styles. Stop for a picnic, a walk, or a giddy ride on a swing at Winn Park, at Peachtree Circle and Lafayette Drive. Follow a scenic street called the Prado to Piedmont Avenue. If you get confused by the labyrinthine street pattern, ask a resident for the way out. Even they get lost in here sometimes.

The ◆ **Atlanta Botanical Garden** (404–876–5859), on sixty acres of Piedmont Park at Piedmont Avenue and the Prado, is the city's newest patch of green. Take your time strolling through formal gardens and rose gardens, a Japanese garden, and a fifteen-acre hardwood forest with a marked walking trail. Numerous state, regional, and national flower shows are held in the Day Building at the entrance. The Botanical Garden's showplace and

2

centerpiece is the $5-million Dorothy Chapman Fuqua Conservatory, which boasts 16,000 square feet of tropical, desert, Mediterranean, and endangered plants. On weekdays from 11:30 A.M. to 1:30 P.M., sandwiches, salads, desserts, and soft drinks are sold in the courtyard of the Day Building. There's also a gift shop with seeds, bulbs, planters, and how-to books. The Garden is open Tuesday through Sunday 9:00 A.M. to 7:00 P.M. Adults are $6.00; senior citizens and ages 6 to 12, $3.00; children 6 and under, free.

After visiting the Botanical Garden, you could spend the rest of the day in ❖ **Piedmont Park.** Facilities include tennis courts, a swimming pool, softball fields, playgrounds, and jogging, hiking, and biking paths. Most of the park is closed to auto traffic. Skate Escape (404–892–1292), across from the park at 1086 Piedmont Avenue, will rent you a bike or a pair of roller skates.

The **Buckhead neighborhood,** off Peachtree Street/Road about 6 miles due north of downtown, has long been Atlanta's most splendid residential enclave. West of Peachtree Road, follow the green and white "Scenic Drive" markers past Spanish and Italian villas, French chateaux, Old English Tudors, white-columned Greek Revivals, Georgians, even Japanese-style show-places that preside over immense lawns and great stands of trees and flowing shrubbery. Some of the most beautiful homes are on West Paces Ferry, Andrews, Habersham, Blackland, Valley, and Tuxedo Roads.

You'll have a better understanding of what makes Atlanta the kind of city it is after a day at the ❖ **Atlanta History Center** (404–814–4000). The tree-shaded, thirty-acre sanctuary at 3101 Andrews Drive includes three fascinating attractions: the insightful and very-well-done Museum of Atlanta History; the circa-1836 "plantation plain" Tullie Smith Farmstead; and the Swan House, an opulent Italian-Palladian villa, built in 1926 and appointed with European and Asian furnishings and set among formal gardens and terraced fountains. Open daily. Adults are $7.00; ages 65 and over and students 18 and over with ID, $5.00; ages 6–17, $4.00; and under age 6, free.

❖ **Zoo Atlanta,** in Grant Park, 3 miles east of downtown (404) 624–5600, is another fun way to spend a day. The most popular area is the Ford African Rainforest, a natural habitat for families of silverback mountain gorillas. The king of the hill is Willie B., who spent almost thirty years in a solitary indoor cage before being released into his new home. He's now a proud papa several times over. Open daily. Adults are $7.50; seniors, $6.50; ages 3–11, $5.50; and 2 and under are free.

Also in Grant Park, the **Cyclorama** is a colossal painting-in-the-round capturing a crucial hour in the Civil War Battle of Atlanta. It's open daily. Phone (404) 656–7625 for information. Adults are $6.00; senior citizens, $5.00; and children, $3.00.

The ✦ **Georgia Governors Mansion** (404–261–1776), near the Historical Society at 391 West Paces Ferry Road, receives visitors Tuesday through Thursday 10:00 to 11:30 A.M. Public rooms in this modern-day Greek Revival mansion, built in the late 1960s, gleam with museum-quality Federal-period antiques and art. Tours are free.

Georgia's nineteenth-century poet Sidney Lanier sang the praises of the Chattahoochee River in his idyllic "Song of the Chattahoochee." The river rises in the north Georgia mountains and flows through metropolitan Atlanta on its way to the Gulf of Mexico.

The ✦ **Chattahoochee River National Recreation Area,** a 48-mile stretch of river and gentle rapids flowing between wooded palisades, is the focus for recreational pursuits of all sorts. From spring through fall, Atlantans love to set their rafts, canoes, and kayaks loose in the river for a lazy day of relaxation. Sturdy four-, six-, and eight-person rafts may be rented from Chattahoochee Outdoor Center, 1825 Northridge Road, (404) 395–6851. If rafting isn't your pleasure, you can also spread a picnic, hike, bike, jog, bird-watch, and exercise on the twenty-two-station fitness trail. The park's main entrance is at Highway 41 and the Chattahoochee River bridge. Contact the Park Superintendent, 1978 Island Ford Parkway, Atlanta 30336; (770) 952–4419.

The river's fauna and flora are celebrated at the ✦ **Chattahoochee Nature Center,** 9135 Willeo Road in Roswell, (404) 992–2055. The private, nonprofit natural-science center's exhibits of plants and wildlife, special programs, and workshops are in a tranquil fifty-acre setting by the riverbanks, about 25 miles north of downtown Atlanta. Guided walks on Saturday and Sunday at noon and 2:00 P.M. weave through twenty acres of nature trails and a 1,400-foot boardwalk over the river. You can also pick up a brochure and take a self-guided tour. Make a full day of it with a picnic lunch. The center is open daily 9:00 A.M. to 5:00 P.M. Admission for adults is $2.00; children and senior citizens, $1.00.

The public square and saltbox-style houses of ◆ **Roswell** mirror the Connecticut roots of founder Roswell King, who planned the town in the 1830s. Nowadays the handsome brick buildings, set around a typical New England green, house restaurants and specialty shops. Greek Revival-style **Bulloch Hall** was built in 1840 by Major James Stephens Bulloch. In 1853 the major's daughter Mittie married Theodore Roosevelt of New York in the mansion's parlor. Their son became twenty-sixth president of the United States. Guided tours are given daily (adults, $4.00; senior citizens, $3.00; children ages 6 to 16, $1.00). Call (770) 992–1731.

Also stop at the **Roswell Historical Society,** 227 South Atlanta Street (404–992–1665) for information and a slide show about the town's heritage. Called Allenbrook, the society's saltbox-style headquarters was built in 1845 with brick walls that are 18 inches thick.

Downtown Atlanta's **Woodruff Park** doesn't have a lot of greenery, but on weekdays this open space at Peachtree, Marietta, and Decatur Streets is an A-1 people-watching location. At weekday lunch, the benches and small patches of grass fill up with Georgia State University students, office workers, street preachers, politicians, freelance musicians, and entertainers. Pick up a sack lunch at one of the numerous eateries around the park and sit back and watch the show.

Among the downtown area's ultra-modern skyscrapers are some lovely architectural treasures of yesteryear. The **William-Oliver Building,** on Peachtree Street across from the park, gleams with Art Deco brass elevator doors, ceiling murals, and decorative grillwork. The **Candler Building,** on the park's northern edge, was built in 1904 by Coca-Cola magnate Asa Candler, who spared no expense in embellishing it with marble friezes, brass and woodwork, and a grand staircase.

Gone With the Wind fans may want to see the memorabilia of the movie and book in the **Margaret Mitchell Collection** at the Atlanta Public Library, downtown at Carnegie Way and Forsyth and Peachtree Streets (404–577–6940). The movie made its gala 1939 world premiere across the street at Loew's Grand Theatre, where the Georgia-Pacific skyscraper now rises.

One of the most interesting ways to delve into the city's history is on a tour led by the ◆ **Atlanta Preservation Center** (404–876–2040). The center's half-dozen walking tours from April through October focus on the city's architectural and cultural heritage. The Fox Theatre tour takes you backstage at one of America's last surviving 1920s "picture palaces." Adorned with minarets, Moorish arches, Egyptian hieroglyphics, and a blue-sky ceiling that twinkles with electric stars, the Fox (404–881–2100) hosts a full schedule of touring musicals, concerts of all sorts, and a summertime classic movie festival. It's at 660 Peachtree Street at Ponce de Leon Avenue.

MARTA, the Metropolitan Atlanta Rapid Transit Authority, is an up-to-date way to get around the city. The clean, two-line rapid rail system intersects at Five Points Station downtown and is a swift way of getting to the **Woodruff Arts Center/High Museum of Art** and other attractions. The MARTA bus system is a more comprehensive but much slower way of getting about. Fare for both is $1.50 one way, including transfers; for information call (404) 522–4711.

✛ **Oakland Cemetery,** 248 Oakland Avenue at Memorial Drive, is a book on Atlanta's past, right behind the ultra-modern King Memorial MARTA Station. Established in 1850, Oakland has redbrick walls that enclose a wealth of architectural and cultural heritage. Here is buried *Gone with the Wind* author Margaret Mitchell, struck down by a taxi on her beloved Peachtree Street in 1949. Victorian aristocrats are entombed in templelike mausoleums, embellished with stained glass, gargoyles, and marble busts. You may walk through Confederate and Jewish sections, see the graves of the city's firstborn child and other celebrities, and spread a picnic lunch under the magnolia trees. Open daily. Free tours are conducted on weekends.

A MARTA train to West End Station and a bus connection or 3-block walk will bring you to the ✛ **Wren's Nest,** the Victorian home of Joel Chandler Harris, creator of Br'er Rabbit, Br'er Fox, the Tar Baby, and other delightful critters who roam through his 1880s book *Uncle Remus: His Songs and Sayings*. Rooms are filled with furnishings and mementos of Harris and his family, editions of his book in many languages, and re-creations of his beloved characters. The house got its name when a mother wren decided that Harris's wooden mailbox would be perfect for her brood. The mailbox now has an honored place among the Wren's Nest's treasures. Especially if you have children, try to visit when storytelling sessions are scheduled—usually the last Saturday of the month and daily during the summer. Wren's Nest, at 1050 Ralph David Abernathy Boulevard, (404) 753–7735,

The Wren's Nest

is open Tuesday through Saturday 10:00 A.M. to 4:00 P.M., Sunday 1:00 to 4:00 P.M. Adults are $4.00; senior citizens and teens, $3.00; ages 4 to 12, $2.00.

Children, as well as adults, will enjoy the ❖ **Center for Puppetry Arts** (404–873–3391), on the northern edge of downtown at 1404 Spring Street. The converted redbrick school building houses a fascinating puppetry museum and puts on a year-round program of puppet theatricals, some aimed at youngsters, others tailored for adults.

West of downtown, ❖ **Herndon Home,** at 587 University Place, is a landmark of Black achievement. The dignified Beaux Art–style mansion was built in 1915 by Alonzo Herndon, a former slave who founded Atlanta Life Insurance Company, the nation's largest Black-owned insurance firm. The fifteen rooms showcase his remarkable life. Most of the antique furnishings and family photos are original. The Herndon Home is open Tuesday through Saturday 1:00 to 4:00 P.M. Free admission. For more information call (404) 581–9813.

The ❖ **APEX Museum,** east of downtown Atlanta at 135 Auburn Avenue, (404) 521–APEX, highlights African-American history, culture, and art with permanent and rotating exhibits by local and national artists. Open Tuesday through Saturday 10:00 A.M. to 5:00 P.M. Admission is $3.00 for adults and $2.00 for senior citizens and children 5 and under.

"Sweet Auburn" Avenue was once a main street of Black commercial success. It's now the heart of the ❖ **Martin Luther King Jr. National Historic Site,** which includes the civil rights leader's tomb, his childhood home, the Ebenezer Baptist Church where he preached, and other landmarks. For guided tours phone the National Park Service at (404) 524–1956.

Atlanta's cosmopolitan character is reflected in restaurants whose specialties range from traditional Southern cooking to exotic dishes from around the world. The biggest selections of restaurants dear to locals' hearts are in the neighborhoods of Buckhead—around the junction of Peachtree, Roswell, East and West Paces Ferry Roads, 6 to 8 miles north of downtown—and Virginia/Highland—a reborn older neighborhood extending from Ponce de Leon Avenue north on North Highland Avenue to Virginia Avenue, about 3 to 4 miles northeast of downtown.

If you still pine for the flower-child days of the sixties or feel like dyeing your hair magenta and skateboarding on the sidewalks, ◆ **Little Five Points** is your kind of place. You can be perfectly mainstream and still enjoy an outing in this Southern East Village/SOHO. Around the intersection of Moreland and Euclid Avenues, about 3 miles east of downtown, you'll find several good, inexpensive, ethnic restaurants—Indian, Latin, Jamaican, Cajun, Italian, Mexican—coffee shops, bars with and without live music, and funky shops selling vintage clothing, new and used CDs, and books on astrology, herbal medicine, and other esoteric subjects. Just like the good old days, street musicians perform for your pleasure and spare change.

Much of Atlanta's lively and varied nightlife is also concentrated in Buckhead and Virginia/Highland. Consult the *Weekend* tabloid in Saturday's *Atlanta Journal-Constitution* for clubs and performers.

If you'd like to stay at a homey bed-and-breakfast inn and meet some engaging Atlantans, contact **Bed-and-Breakfast Atlanta,** 1801 Piedmont Avenue, Atlanta 30324, (404) 875–0525; FAX (404) 875–9672. Accommodations are in beautiful private homes, and rates usually include a full breakfast and the opportunity to meet Atlantans on an informal basis.

With a population of more than 500,000, De Kalb is metro Atlanta's second largest county. Amid a patchwork of crowded streets and freeways, shopping malls and subdivisions, you'll find many off-the-beaten-path attractions.

The thriving Asian community has changed the face of Chamblee, Doraville, and other northeast De Kalb County towns and has given the area the nickname ◆ **De Kalb County's "Little Asia."** For those who enjoy ◆ the exotic tastes of the Orient, there's an abundance of authentic Korean, Chinese, Thai, Vietnamese, and Japanese restaurants and food markets. At **Koreatown Plaza,** a modern shopping center at 5302 Buford Highway, Doraville, you'll find imported clothes, food, and gifts, as well as **Yen Jing,** (404–454–6688), a Chinese restaurant with a distinctive Korean spin. You'll also find a variety of Southeast Asian shops at **Chinatown Square,** 5399 New Peachtree Road, Chamblee, where the **Oriental Pearl** (404–986–9866) has one of the area's best dim sum brunches.

Other top-notch eateries in the area include **Garam** (Korean), 5881 Buford Highway, Doraville, (404) 454–9198; **Ben Thuy** (Vietnamese), 5095–F, Buford Highway, Doraville (404) 454–9046; **Honto** (Hong-style Chinese seafood), 3295 Chamblee-Dunwoody

Road, Chamblee, (404) 458–8088; **Sakana-Ya** (Japanese), 6241-A Peachtree Industrial Boulevard, Doraville, (404) 458–0558; and **Taste of Thai,** 5775 Jimmy Carter Boulevard, Norcross (in nearby Gwinnett County), (404) 662–8575.

From downtown Atlanta follow Ponce de Leon Avenue east to Clifton Road and go north to the junction of Clifton and North Decatur Roads, where you'll see signs to various university areas. On the Emory University campus, about 2 miles from downtown Decatur on North Decatur and Oxford Roads, is the ✦ **Michael C. Carlos Emory University Museum of Art and Archae-ology** (404–727–4282). This small gem holds a trove of antiquities and modern art. On the first floor, you'll see Greek and Roman coins, amphorae, and an Egyptian mummy with a gilded face. Upstairs are displays of European, American, and Oriental art. A $3.00 donation is requested. The museum is open Tuesday through Saturday 11:00 A.M. to 4:30 P.M.

Across from the campus, you'll find a string of student-oriented shops and eateries such as the popular **Everybody's** and **Jagger's.**

A granite hulk 825 feet high and 6 miles around, with scores of attractions and six million yearly visitors, is hardly off the beaten path. However, many Stone Mountain Park visitors miss ✦ **Stone Mountain Village.** Outside the state park's gates, the Village's Main Street has a nineteenth-century covered side-walk and 3 blocks of stores stocked with old books, Civil War artifacts, handicrafts, geodes, and oddities. You can get a haircut in an old-fashioned barber shop, buy an ice cream, a sandwich, or a full meal. Take a MARTA bus to the Village from downtown Atlanta or make an adventure of the trip by chugging out on the New Georgia Railroad's steam-powered train.

Antiques lovers and fellow junkers can have a ball in a big assortment of shops clustered in the northeast De Kalb County town of ✦ **Chamblee.** Take MARTA's North Line train to the Chamblee Station and walk 2 blocks north on Peachtree Road. Around the Peachtree Road/Broad Street junction, explore such fun emporiums as **Moose Breath Trading Co.** (770–455–0518), Broad Street Antique Mall (770–458–6316), and the Whippoorwill Co. (770–455–8357).

Decatur, the usually tranquil DeKalb County seat (population 22,000), will be bristling with round-the-clock activity during the Summer Olympics when it hosts several thousand members of the Irish delegation. The Irish will put on entertainment and cultural exhibits in their home base in the Old DeKalb County Courthouse/DeKalb Historical Society, at Clairemont and Ponce de Leon Avenues.

Before, during, and after the Games, many budget-conscious travelers will find Decatur a welcome retreat. Many savvy visitors have already discovered ❖ **The Atlanta Dream Hostel.** The metro area's only hostel, the Dream has 300 beds in mostly dormitory setups in groups of revamped homes and offices near the Decatur Courthouse Square. It's $12 a night, including kitchen privileges, a big garden, an Elvis shrine, and a "Barbie Doll" girls' dorm. Some single and double rooms are available. It's a quick walk from Decatur's MARTA rail station—which links you with the rest of the metro area—and cheap eats and entertainment. The Dream is located at 222 East Howard Avenue, Decatur 30030, (404) 370–0380.

A block from the hostel, **The Great Southeastern Freight Room,** 301 East Howard Avenue, (404) 378–5365, serves bar food, drinks, and live folk/bluegrass/Cajun/acoustic music in Decatur's old wooden train depot. Just across the tracks, **The Our Way Cafe** (404–373–6665) serves huge plates of simply wonderful, rock-bottom cheap Southern homecooking at weekday lunchtime. The squash souffle is to die for! **Eddie's Attic,** a walk-up on the Courthouse Square, 515 North McDonough Street, (404) 377–4976, is one of the most convivial places in the metro area to hear popular local acoustic groups. Bar food, drinks, beer, and wine are available.

What do you do on a rainy day in Atlanta? Rain or shine, you could spend all of it at the ❖ **Fernbank Museum of Natural History** and the neighboring Fernbank Science Center. The Natural History Museum's feature attractions include the hands-on "Walk Through Time in Georgia," Children's Discovery Rooms, an IMAX Theater, lifelike dinosaurs, and changing national and international exhibitions. Open daily. Adults are $9.50; students and ages 65 and over, $8.50; ages 3–12, $6.50. The IMAX Theater may be seen without the museum or on a package ticket with the museum. The Fernbank Museum is at 767 Clifton Road between Decatur and downtown Atlanta. Call (404) 370–0960 for more information.

The ❖ **Fernbank Science Center,** set in a sixty-five-acre forest threaded with walking trails, has a 500-seat planetarium

offering seasonal looks at the heavens. You may also check out
far-flung galaxies through the Southeast's largest telescope. Other
exhibits focus on Georgia's rich plant and animal life. Fernbank is
open daily and charges only for planetarium shows: $2.00 adults,
$1.00 students. The Fernbank Science Center is at 156 Heaton
Park Drive, (404) 378–4311.

MONKS, A MOUNTAIN, AND GONE WITH THE WIND

❖ **Yellow River Wildlife Game Ranch** is a peaceful place in
the woods in the midst of south Gwinnett County's suburban
explosion. Just off very busy Highway 78, 3 miles east of Stone
Mountain Park, the twenty-four-acre privately owned nature preserve is home for dozens of free-roaming brown deer, huggable
bunnies, goats, sheep, coyotes, ducks and geese, pigs and porcu-
pines, foxes, wolves, donkeys, a skunk named William T. Sherman, and a spring-forecasting groundhog named Robert E. Lee.

Deer are Yellow River's self-appointed reception committee.
You're no sooner on the tree-shaded walking trail than whole
families of gentle does, bucks, and fawns are ambling up for
handouts of bread and crackers and a scratch behind the ears.
During summer, fragile newborn fawns are an especially appeal-
ing sight. Lambs, piglets, baby ducks, and goat kids are also very
much in the spotlight.

Small children get a kick out of the Bunnie Burrows, an
enclosed area where rabbits of all sizes and colors seem to enjoy
being petted and hand fed raw carrots and celery.

What's purportedly the largest herd of American buffalo east of
the Mississippi roams a back meadow. Black bear, bobcats, mountain lions, foxes, and wolves are secured in open-air enclosures,
out of the reach of little fingers. If you spread a picnic lunch in a
grove by the Yellow River, expect some "deer" friends to drop by
for a treat.

You may reserve Yellow River's **Birthday House** for your
youngster's special day or for a family reunion or other group
activity. Yellow River Wildlife Game Ranch, at 4525 Interstate 78
in Lilburn (770–972–6643) is open daily in the summer 9:30 A.M.
to 9:00 P.M. The rest of the year it closes at 6.00 P.M. Admission
for adults is $5.00; ages 3 to 11, $4.00; 2 and under, no charge.

The ❖ **Sugar Hill Municipal Golf Course** (8 miles north

of the Suwanee exit off I–85, (770–271–0519) is a sweet layout for those who'd like to play like the pros but have an amateur's budget. Spread over 300 acres at the north Gwinnett County town of Sugar Hill, the well-maintained par-72, 18-hole course offers plenty of challenges as it swoops up and down hills and around six lakes and forty-five traps.

Amid the burgeoning suburbs of Rockdale County, a short drive off the busy lanes of I–20, about 25 miles east of downtown Atlanta, the ❖ **Monastery of the Holy Ghost** is a place of inordinate peacefulness. Since the late 1940s, Benedictine Trappist monks have dwelt and prayed in this cloistered sanctuary at 2625 Highway 212 in Conyers (770–483–8705). The Spanish Gothic-style buildings, even the stained glass in the main church, are all products of their labors.

Men and women may attend Sunday morning mass in the church, which is highlighted by the monks' chants and prayers. Men may make retreats at the modern guest house nearby. A small shop sells bread, cheese, jam, religious items, and produce and herbs grown in the monastery's fields. You may also bring a picnic lunch to tables that sit by a lake beside the cloister.

The abbey does not observe a strict rule of silence, and most monks may converse with visitors.

Just east of Conyers on I–20 is Covington in Newton County. Fans of TV's *In the Heat of the Night* will recognize many of the show's locations around the **Covington** courthouse square. Many beautiful white-columned homes are on the tree-shaded streets radiating from the square.

You'll also find a trove of antebellum treasures around nearby **Oxford College of Emory University,** which welcomed its first freshman class in 1839.

Twenty miles southeast of downtown Atlanta, via Highway 155, ❖ **Panola Mountain State Conservation Park** is a peaceful 585-acre day-use park where you may have a walk in the woods, enjoy a picnic, and wonder at a 100-acre granite outcropping that's been part of the Henry County landscape for about a million years. The lichen-covered monadnock is part of a major belt of granite, most dramatically evidenced by Stone Mountain, a few miles away.

Stop first at the park's Nature Center for information on trails leading through the woodlands and around the mountain. Meandering through hardwood and pine forests, the 1¼-mile Micro-watershed Trail is a moderately strenuous course. Several stations along the way have benches and markers describing the park's fauna and flora. At the base of Panola Mountain, a three-acre pond is alive with turtles, frogs, fish, and small reptiles.

The ¾-mile Rock Outcrop Trail takes you through the woods to an overlook on one of the mountain's major outcroppings. On Saturday and Sunday afternoons, park naturalists conduct walks and give talks at the small amphitheater near the Nature Center. Picnic tables are located near rest rooms and soft drinks machines. Pets on leashes may be walked in the picnic area but aren't allowed on the nature trails.

The park is open daily from 8:00 A.M. to sundown. There is a $2.00 parking fee. Contact the superintendent, Stockbridge 30281, (770) 389–7801.

South of the park, via Highway 155, you'll find small cafes and shops around the pretty little courthouse square in **McDonough.** On the third Saturday of May, the Geranium Festival fills the square with arts, crafts, and entertainment. The popular **Indian Springs State Park** is a short drive south of McDonough.

Bargain lovers should put the Spalding County seat of **Griffin** high on their shopping lists. The textile town of 20,000, on Highways 19/41, 40 miles south of Atlanta, has some especially tempting values in towels and socks.

Dundee Towel Shop (770–227–4165) is an attractive, modern outlet for Dundee Corporation's products. First-run and irregular bath towels, beach towels, kitchen towels, et al., are available in a big variety of styles, colors, and fabrics at prices much lower than you'll find at retail stores. The shop, at 1440 North Expressway, Griffin 30223, is open Monday through Saturday 9:00 A.M. to 6:00 P.M. Major credit cards are accepted.

Spalding Knitting Mills Sock Shop (770–227–4362) has the answer to virtually all your hosiery needs. Aisles are jammed with colorful argyles, athletic socks, dress socks, heavy-duty work socks, as well as pantyhose, sweat shirts, and other items made by major manufacturers. Irregulars, with all but impossible to discern blemishes, go for at least half the price you'd normally pay. First-run items are more expensive, but still very much a bargain. It's open Monday through Saturday 8:30 A.M. to 5:30 P.M. No credit cards accepted. On East Broad Street, across from the red-brick Spalding Mills, a block from the center

14

of town. Write to P.O. Box 593, Griffin 30223.

❖ **Cherokee Rose Shooting Resort,** P.O. Box 509, Griffin 30224, (770) 228–CLAY, is one of the first places in Georgia to offer the European sport of "sporting clays." Guests "hunting" on wooded trails fire at clay discs that simulate the movements of birds and game. The resort also has a pistol and rifle range, skeet and trap shooting, a restaurant, and a comfortably rustic lodge that sleeps six.

You can sleep in antebellum history at two unique Griffin area bed-and-breakfasts. **Double Cabins Plantation,** a Doric-columned 1842 Greek Revival home lived in by seven generations of builder Shateen Mitchell's descendants, is set among gardens, old trees, and pre–Civil War outbuildings. Five guest rooms in the main house have many original furnishings and period pieces. Two have private baths. Rates are $85 for a double, including full breakfast. Group tours are available. Contact Mrs Douglas Holberg, 3335 Jackson Road, Griffin 30223, (770) 227–6611.

Inn Scarlett's Footsteps, at 138 Hill Street, Concord 30206, (770) 495–9012 and (800) 886–7355, is a must for *Gone With the Wind* fans. Innkeepers K. C. and Vern Bassham, former Ohioans, have turned a majestic white-columned mansion, a "Twelve Oaks" lookalike, into a nostalgic trip through the novel and the movie. Five bedrooms are named for Scarlett, Rhett, Melanie, Ashley, and Gerald. Each has appropriate decor and a private bath. The Museum Room displays thousands of pieces of *GWTW* memorabilia collected by the Basshams. Rates are $79 for a double, including full Southern breakfast. Group tours are by appointment at $5.00 a person.

LEWIS GRIZZARD AND ANTEBELLUM NEWNAN

Coweta and Fayette Counties, on metro Altlanta's southwest periphery, are perfect for a one-day getaway from the big city, and they have more than enough to keep you happily occupied for much longer than that.

Take I–85 exit 9, 40 miles south of Atlanta, and follow Bullsboro Drive/Highway 34 into downtown Newnan. First stop at the **Coweta County Convention & Visitors Bureau,** 22 East Broad Street, (770) 254–2627 and (800) 8–COWETA. They'll fill you in on every place to see, do, eat, and sleep in and around the city of 12,000. Be sure to pick up an ❖ **Antebellum Newnan**

Driving Tour of Homes guide, which describes twenty-three pre–Civil War landmarks. Many of the homes welcome visitors during the annual **Tour of Homes and Arts and Crafts Show** the third week of April. Before your driving tour, park around the majestic old courthouse in the center of the square and browse the many antiques, gift, and book shops that lure locals away from the ubiquitous malls on the outskirts. **The Alamo Gift Shop** used to be Newnan's first-run movie house. Owner Elizabeth Crain spent many childhood hours in the old theater, and she's left the Alamo's stage and balcony for old-time's sake. If you're addicted to hot stuff—and consider no meal is fit to eat until it's doused with liquid fire—stop by **The Redneck Gourmet and Deli,** (770) 251–0092. Their array of hot sauces includes some so ferocious they come equipped with an eyedropper. At lunchtime downtown workers line up at the lunch counter for the Redneck's nonlethal hot and cold sandwiches, salads, and soups. You can pour your own "poison" from the selection on the counter.

If you're a fan of the late syndicated humor columnist Lewis Grizzard—a Coweta native son—you'll find all his books and tapes at **Scott's Books,** (770) 253–2960. Owner Earlene Scott was a close friend of Grizzard's, and she's always happy to share her memories. A Grizzard museum, described below, is in the small community of Moreland, south of Newnan.

General Wheeler's Mess Tent, off the Square at 9 Perry Street, (770) 253–8874, bills itself as "Georgia's Only Living Civil War Cafe." Owner Russ Styanoff, an ardent Civil War enthusiast, named his place for Confederate Gen. Joseph A. Wheeler, whose cavalry defeated Union troups at Brown's Mill crossroads in 1864 and saved Newnan from destruction. You'll know you've arrived by the Confederate flag and military mess tent out front. Inside, the old house is festooned with flags, weapons, uniforms, and portraits of Wheeler and other Southern heroes. They lend their names to menu items: "The Stonewall Jackson—the finest Angus roast beef of the valley divided into two corps will race with lightning speed to defeat your hunger." Gen. Wheeler, a meat-and-potatoes kind of guy, would be scratching his beard over his namesake, fettuccine Wheeler-Alfredo. The day-long Sunday buffet attracts a big after-church crowd. The Old South really comes alive on Friday and Saturday nights when "The Politically Incorrect Players," in Confederate regalia, sing and play "The Greatest

16

Hits of 1863." Lunch and dinner are served daily in the spring and summer, Thursday to Monday in the fall and winter.

Several of Newnan's antebellum and Victorian mansions welcome bed-and-breakfast guests. **The Parrot Camp Soucy Home and Gardens,** 155 Greenville Street, Newnan 30263, (770) 502–0676, literally stops traffic in its tracks. The stunning Second Empire–style mansion, built in 1842 and redesigned in 1884, with a wealth of gables, a wide veranda, and intricate exterior millwork, is straight out of the Gilded Age. The fantasy is carried out inside, where former Californians Helen and Rick Cousin have created a sumptuous bed-and-breakfast. Four guest rooms are furnished with Victorian antiques, canopy and half-tester beds, fireplaces, and modern private baths. Guests enjoy four acres of formal gardens, a heated spa and outdoor pool, and a full gourmet breakfast. Doubles run $105–$165.

The Old Garden Inn, at 51 Temple Avenue, Newnan 30263, (770) 304–0594 and (800) 731–5011, has three cheerful guest rooms in a white-columned Greek Revival mansion. Each has a different decorative theme. One has a private entrance popular with smokers who can step outside and puff away. Breakfast, included in rates of $75–$89, features owner Patti Girondi's sweet potato biscuits and cheese grits souffle.

The late syndicated humor columnist Lewis Grizzard wrote fondly about growing up in tiny Moreland (population 450), on Highway 29 a few minutes south of Newnan. In appreciation, townsfolk have opened ◆ **The Lewis Grizzard Museum** (770) 304–1490. In a turn-of-the-century doctor's office, the small museum displays his many books, photos, battered manual typewriters, and memorabilia. If you're a true fan, be here the first Saturday of April when thousands of his friends and fans come for the Annual Lewis Grizzard Storytelling and Barbecue. The museum is open Saturday and Sunday. Other times, Bill Myatt, who runs the gift shop next door, will let you in. Adults are $2.00, ages 6–12, $1.00

Just across a small park, Coweta Countians have restored the birthplace of novelist ◆ **Erskine Caldwell.** The author of *God's Little Acre* and *Tobacco Road* was born in "The Manse" in 1903 when his father was a Presbyterian pastor here. The family left when Caldwell was five years old, and he never lived here as an adult. But the simple frame house is very much as he knew it. Biographical exhibits, personal items, copies of his books in sev-

17

eral languages, and a video trace the career of the author who died in 1987. The house is open 1:00 to 4:00 P.M. Saturday and Sunday and by appointment. Adults are $2.00, ages 6–12, $1.00. Call (770) 251–4438 for more information. You can go directly to Moreland from I–85 exit 8 and driving south on Highway 29.

Catalpa Plantation and Herb Farm, 2295 Old Poplar Road, Newnan 30263, is the closest antebellum plantation to Atlanta still on its original site. Built between 1835 and 1840, the Federal-Vernacular-style main house commanded 1,000 acres of cotton fields. Authentically restored by Rod and Renae Smith and furnished with period antiques, the mansion is open for tours by appointment. Renae's Herb Shop, adjacent to the house, sells dried aromatic herbs, fresh culinary herbs, seasonal wreaths, antiques, books, vinegars, and other gifts. Call (800) 697–1835 for mansion tours and Herb Shop hours. The Smiths are also custodians of **The Homeplace,** 1262 Bob Smith Road, Newnan 30263, (770) 253–3806, a bed-and-breakfast in an 1820s "plantation plain" farmhouse. Three bedrooms and double parlors have original wood floors, walls and ceilings, mantels, and wainscoting. Breakfast is included in the $85–$110 rates.

Senoia, a drowsy little Coweta County town on Highway 85, 40 miles south of Atlanta, is like a delightful trip through Norman Rockwell–land. As you're strolling down Main Street, townsfolk smile and inquire politely about your family and your health.

◆ **The Buggy Shop Museum** (770–599–1222), on Senoia's 1-block Main Street, was originally a collection of old-time memorabilia assembled by the late James Baggarly, Sr. Since "Mr. Jim's" death, his son, Walter Baggarly, has refurbished an early 1900s Coca-Cola bottling plant and given it a new name. The eclectic horde includes nineteenth-century buggies and wagons, a 1925 Model A Ford James Baggarly drove on his rural postal route, a working Edison record player, Native American arrowheads, vintage farm implements, early Coca-Cola bottles and signs, a player piano, an early 1900s gasoline pump, and many, many other nostalgic treasures. It's open Friday to Sunday, other days by appointment. Adults are $2.00, children, $1.00.

Also on Main Street, **Hutchinson Hardware** is another revered Senoia institution of long standing. Painted bright blue, with a parade of tall arched windows and doors, the building started out as a Ford dealership in the 1920s and became a hardware store early in World War II, when the Hutchinson's supply of Fords went dry. The aisles are stacked with anything you'd want for fishing, hunting, canning, serious farming and hobby gardening, or building a house or barn and keeping them in proper order. Owner Jimmy Hutchinson is used to hearing townspeople say: "I know what I need is in here somewhere" and "If Hutchinson ain't got it, I don't need it."

Senoia has two beguiling places to spend the night. The **Culpepper House** dates back to 1871, when it was built by Dr. John Addy, a returning Civil War veteran. Four guest rooms, two with private baths, are furnished with Victorian antiques. Public areas shine with gingerbread trim, stained glass, and pocket doors. A full Southern breakfast served in the stone-hearthed kitchen is included in rates of $75 double with private or shared bath. Write to 35 Broad Street, Senoia 30276, or call (770) 599–8182.

The **Veranda Inn** (770–599–3905), built as a hotel at the turn of the century, was one of the first places hereabouts to be electrified. Now operated by Bobby and Jan Boal, the Veranda sleeps up to sixteen guests in rooms blessedly free of televisions and telephones. For entertainment, guests step onto the spacious front veranda and avail themselves of rocking chairs and a porch swing. A double room with private bath is $90–$110 and comes with a whopping big Southern breakfast. The mailing address is The Veranda, Box 177, Senoia 30276–0177.

Four miles north of Senoia, at the junction of Highways 85 and 74, stands ❖ **Starr's Mill,** one of Georgia's most photographed landmarks. One look at the 200-year-old red frame mill, hard by a pond and waterfall, and you'll be rushing for your camera, too. When you go, be sure to bring along a blanket and picnic.

Melear's (770–461–7180), on Highway 85 at Fayetteville's southern limits, has been serving delicious barbecue and Brunswick stew for more than thirty years. A big plateful costs under $6.00. During the short wait, amuse yourselves with the owner's collection of pig pottery and portraits. Open for lunch and dinner Monday through Saturday.

SHERMAN MEETS THE SUBURBS

Since 1968 the picturesque rapids of Sweetwater Creek and the adjacent hardwood and piny woodlands have been the heart of

❖ **Sweetwater Creek Conservation Park,** a peaceful day-use state park. A short drive off I–20, 15 miles west of downtown Atlanta, the park serves the populace of rapidly growing Douglas County and many others who find it a delightful retreat from the hurly-burly of big-city life.

The ghostly ruins of the **New Manchester Manufacturing Company,** a Civil War–era enterprise torched by General William T. Sherman's troops, stands by the churning rapids, which provided the company with power to produce uniforms for the Confederate army. During the summer, kick off your shoes and join others wading in the swift, cool waters. Be careful of the slick patches of moss covering the rocks.

Five miles of nature trails lead you through the woods beside the creek. A 250-acre reservoir is stocked with bass, catfish, and bream, which you can fry in a pan and serve on one of the park's picnic tables. The park is open daily from 8:00 A.M. to sundown. There is a $2.00 parking fee. Contact the superintendent, Lithia Springs 30057, (770) 732–5871.

With 450,000 residents, affluent Cobb is one of the nation's fastest growing counties and the northwest flagship of the Atlanta metropolitan area. Off the well-beaten paths of freeways and around the corner from high-rise hotels, glitzy shopping galleries, and trendy eateries, you'll find fascinating historic sites, charming town squares, and outdoor recreation.

After the fall of Chattanooga in late 1863, the Confederates grudgingly fell back to Kennesaw Mountain, 25 miles north of Atlanta and the site of ❖ **Kennesaw Mountain National Battlefield Park.** For two weeks in June 1864, 60,000 soldiers dug into the wooded flanks of the 1,808-foot mountain. When a series of assaults failed to dislodge the Southerners, Union commander General William T. Sherman executed a flanking strategy, which forced the Confederates to leave the mountain and retreat to Atlanta.

Stop first at the National Park Service Visitors Center and view the slide presentation and exhibits. Outside are some of the cannons that took part in the battle. From Monday through Friday you may drive your car up a paved road to a parking area 200 yards below the summit. From there take an easy walk through the woods studded with cannons, earthworks, and markers telling the story of the battle. On Saturday and Sunday the mountain road is open only to a free shuttle bus that makes the trip every half hour. In fair weather many visitors hike at least one way on an easy 1-mile trail. If you've the stamina, you can extend your hike from the Kennesaw summit 4 miles to **Cheatham Hill** and 7 miles to **Kolb's Farm,** other principal battlegrounds in the Kennesaw theater. The two areas are also accessible by car.

Picnic tables, grills, and rest rooms are in a grove of trees near the visitors center parking area. The park, about 4½ miles west of I–75 exit 116, is open Monday through Friday 8:30 A.M. to 5:00 P.M.; Saturday and Sunday to 6:00 P.M. Contact the superintendent, P.O. Box 1167, Marietta 30061, (770) 427–4686.

The **locomotive General** is another tangible souvenir of the Civil War. On April 12, 1862, Union raiders stole the locomotive as it sat in the Kennesaw depot. Their plan to decimate Confederate rail lines as they drove north to Chattanooga was foiled after a 100-mile chase. Eight of the raiders were hanged; the adventure was dramatized in the Disney movie *The Great Locomotive Chase.* The General is now permanently parked in the ✤ **Big Shanty Museum** in the small town of Kennesaw, 3½ miles from Kennesaw Mountain. You may also see a twelve-minute slide show and Civil War weapons and artifacts. It's open daily. Admission for adults is $2.50; children, $1.00. Before leaving town browse through the piles of weapons, uniforms, old photos, and books at **Wildman's Civil War Surplus Store,** across from the museum. It's run by Civil War enthusiast "Wildman" Dent Myers.

✤ **Marietta Town Square,** officially called Glover Park, is a charming nineteenth-century microcosm of mellow brick buildings, shady streets, and gingerbread Victorian homes. The grassy park in the center of the square has been landscaped as a restful Victorian green, with a gazebo, playground, a fountain, and plenty of benches for quiet relaxation. Shops around the square are stocked with antiques, art and handicrafts, jewelry, and apparel. The square also boasts several good restaurants. **Schillings on the Square** (770–428–9520) has a downstairs pub with sandwiches and light fare and a white tablecloth upstairs dining room featuring lamb, veal, steaks, and seafood.

Stop first at the Marietta Welcome Center, in the restored Western & Atlantic Railway Depot just off the square (404–429–1115), for information and directions for a walking tour of the city's lovely antebellum and Victorian neighborhoods. You can stay in a charming bed-and-breakfast by contacting Victorian Inns of Marietta/Atlanta, 192 Church Street, Marietta 30060, (770) 426–1881. To get to the Marietta square from Highway 41, go west on Roswell Street about 1 mile from the Big Chicken, a local landmark.

Smack in the midst of Cobb County's burgeoning suburbia, ◆ **Rocky Pine Ranch**—1231 Shallowford Road, Marietta 30066, (770) 926–3795—is like a little corner of the Old West, offering you the opportunity to trail ride over seventy-five acres of woodlands and rolling countryside. You can hire a horse by the hour, completely outfitted for Western-style riding. And don't worry about a guide, the horses know every inch of the terrain.

When Georgia's summer heat and humidity get you down, take a refreshing plunge into the **Atlanta Ocean,** a big, boisterous wave pool at White Water Park (770–424–WAVE), on Highway 41 at Marietta. Open daily from May through August, the park has more than thirty attractions: the Ocean, a 750,000-gallon pool that whips up 4-foot waves; a variety of water slides; and special areas for the small fry.

For other water-oriented recreation, try **Lake Allatoona,** which borders Cobb County on the north, and the **Chattahoochee River,** which Cobb shares on the south with Fulton County and Atlanta.

◆ **Pickett's Mill Battlefield,** 5 miles northeast of Dallas, should be high on Civil War buffs' "must-do" list. The battlefield is much as it was when blue and gray troops fought here during the Battle of Atlanta campaign. Living-history programs demonstrate cooking, weapons firing, and military drills of the Civil War era. Artifacts and exhibits are in the interpretive center/visitors center. The battlefield is at Mt. Tabor Road, Dallas 30132, (770) 433–7850. Admission is $2.00 for adults and $1.00 for students. Open Tuesday through Sunday.

SOUTHWEST GEORGIA

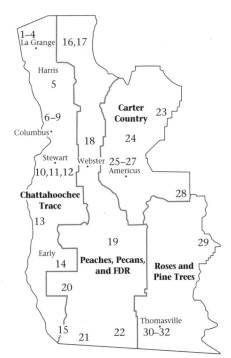

1. Bellevue Mansion
2. Chattahoochee Valley Art Association
3. West Point Lake
4. Hogan's Heroes
5. Day Butterfly Center/ Callaway Gardens
6. Columbus Riverwalk
7. *Chattahoochee Princess*
8. National Infantry Museum
9. Confederate Naval Museum/Columbus Museum
10. Providence Canyon State Park
11. Florence Marina State Park
12. Westville
13. George T. Bagby State Park
14. Kolomoki Mounds State Historic Park
15. Lake Seminole
16. Little White House

17. Franklin D. Roosevelt State Park
18. Pasaquan Folk Art Compound
19. Chehaw Wild Animal Park
20. "Swamp Gravy"
21. Climax Swine Time
22. Rattlesnake Roundup
23. American Camellia Society
24. Montezuma
25. Andersonville National Cemetery and Historic Site
26. Windsor Hotel
27. Jimmy Carter National Historic Site
28. Georgia Veterans Memorial State Park
29. Georgia Agrirama
30. Lapham-Patterson House
31. Pebble Hill Plantation
32. Thomasville Rose Garden

Southwest Georgia

Chattahoochee Trace

La Grange, a pretty town of 25,000 near the Georgia-Alabama border, was named in honor of the Marquis de Lafayette's French estate, which accounts for the bronze likeness of the Marquis in the center of downtown Lafayette Square. Away from the square, regal white-columned mansions preside over well-tended lawns, gardens, and tree-shaded streets.

◆ **Bellevue Mansion,** 204 Ben Hill Street, (706) 884–1832, was the stately Greek Revival home of U.S. Senator and acclaimed orator Benjamin Harvey Hill. Built in the early 1850s, the home is an architectural treasure inside and out, filled with magnificent furnishings and artworks. It's the La Grange area's favorite wedding venue. Open Tuesday through Saturday 10:00 A.M. to noon and 2:00 to 5:00 P.M., Bellevue charges an admission fee of $1.50.

Lamar Dodd Art Center (706–882–2911), on the neighboring La Grange College campus, is a strikingly modern museum displaying changing regional and national exhibitions and a permanent collection of American Indian art. It is open Monday through Friday 10:00 A.M. to 4:00 P.M.; Saturday and Sunday, 1:00 to 4:00 P.M.

The ◆ **Chattahoochee Valley Art Association** (706–882–3267), near Lafayette Square at 112 Hines Street, displays paintings, sculpture, and decorative arts in a restored 1890s jail building. It's open Monday through Friday 9:00 A.M. to 5:00 P.M., Saturday until 1:00 P.M.

◆ **West Point Lake,** a mammoth 26,000-acre inland sea a few minutes from downtown La Grange, offers plenty of opportunities for fishing, boating, swimming, waterskiing, and sunbathing. Contact the West Point Lake Resource Manager, P.O. Box 574, West Point 31833, (706) 645–2937. The lake's commercial outlets include Highland Marina, P.O. Box 1644, La Grange 30241, (706) 882–3437, where you may rent fishing boats and go after the lake's channel catfish and white and largemouth bass. Also at the marina, you may rent a houseboat or stay in a campground or furnished cottage. The lake is a U.S. Army Corps of Engineers impoundment of the Chattahoochee River, which forms most of the Georgia-Alabama border.

In the mood for a hot dog? **Charlie Joseph's** has been serving them up, and Troup Countians have been gobbling them up, since 1920, when Charlie's opened as a fruit stand in downtown La Grange. They've been at 128 Bull Street (706–884–5416) since 1946. You can have your dog with just plain mustard and onions, or dressed up with slaw, chili, cheese, relish, and other fixin's. They also have hamburgers and sandwiches and breakfast-time egg and cheese sandwiches. Charlie's second location, 2238 West Point Road (706–884–0379), serves breakfast, lunch, and early dinner. Both Charlies are open Monday to Saturday.

As you drive Highway 29 from La Grange to Hogansville and pass a humble-looking cinder-block restaurant called ◆ **Hogan's Heroes** (706–637–4953), don't think your nose is deceiving you. Instead of the aromas of barbecue and fried chicken you'd expect in a small west-Georgia textile town, what assails you are the intoxicating fragrances of oregano, thyme, garlic, rosemary, calamari, and veal scallopini.

Hogan's Heroes owner/chef Jeff Spader learned Italian cooking in his native New Jersey. He brought his skills to Hogansville in the late 1980s and has been doing land office building ever since. Regulars flock from across west Georgia and east Alabama to sample his pasta, veal, chicken, and seafood dishes draped in rich, hearty sauces. You can usually find a table during weekday lunchtime, but savvy regulars make dinner reservations at least two weeks ahead. The restaurant has a good selection of wines by the bottle and glass. Prices are moderate.

If you fancy antiques and collectibles, you'll find some good browsing places on **Hogansville's Main Street.** Several old mercantile buildings now sport Depression glass, vintage china and silver, old toys, antique farm implements, and other treasures.

The Fair Oaks at the Grand, 301 East Main Street, Hogansville 30230, (706) 637–5100, is the centerpiece of Main Street's revival. Opened in 1995, the deluxe bed-and-breakfast inn occupies the old Grand Hotel, a two-story frame 1880s traveling salesmen's lodging. Innkeeper Ken Hammock's six guest rooms and four suites have different decorative themes and antiques reflecting their names: "Casablanca," "Peking," "Riviera," etc. Rates are $85 to $125, including breakfast. A French chef directs the kitchen, which serves American/continental meals Monday to Saturday.

Ken Hammock's original **Fair Oaks Inn,** 703 East Main Street, Hogansville 30230, (706) 637–8828, is a stunning 1901 Queen

Anne Victorian loaded with antiques, fireplaces, pocket doors, woodwork, and mantels. Six guest rooms (two sharing a bath) and a large suite with a whirlpool are in the main house. The Carriage House is popular with honeymooners and others seeking seclusion. Guests enjoy formal gardens and an outdoor swimming pool and hot tub. Weekday rates of $50–$85, $65–$110 weekends, include gourmet breakfast and poolside wine and cheese. With all these fragile antiques, no children under 14 are allowed.

Butterflies—thousands of them, in all sizes and colors, from exotic places around the world—are free and on the wing at the ❖ **Day Butterfly Center** at Callaway Gardens in Pine Mountain. Opened to visitors in September 1988, America's first such natural attraction was inspired by similar preserves in Europe and the Orient, with some distinctive Georgia touches. It was named in honor of Cecil Day, late founder of the Days Inns of America motel corporation, and is a year-round, indoor-outdoor experience.

As you walk into an 8,000-square-foot, glass-enclosed "rain forest," you're suddenly caught in clouds of feathery giant swallowtails *(Papilio cresphontes)*, Paris peacock swallowtails *(P. paris)*, green-banded swallowtails *(P. palinurus)*, owl butterflies *(Caligo sp.)*, passion flower butterflies *(Helinconius sp.)*, and a rainbow of other iridescent beauties from the Orient, the Andes, and the South Pacific. Butterflies and tropical birds perch side by side on exotic plants. A waterfall gently spatters. Hummingbirds flit past. Bleeding-heart doves hide in the thick tropical foliage. Indoors, you'll find educational displays and a theater with a film all about the remarkable lives of butterflies.

Outside, the native butterfly garden is cunningly designed to lure homegrown butterflies to ❖ **Callaway Gardens.** If you'd like to have your own butterfly center, Callaway's horticulturists will show you how to plant a "tender trap" in your backyard.

While you're at Callaway Gardens, you may also take a driving tour of the 2,500 acres of gardens planted with 700 varieties of azaleas and more than 450 types of holly, mums, mountain laurel, rhododendron, dogwood, and wildflowers. These may be viewed in their natural habitat, along 13 miles of roads and walking trails, and inside the **John A. Sibley Horticultural Center,** a stunning indoor-outdoor conservatory with pools, cascades, and scores of floral displays that change with the seasons.

Callaway Gardens

Callaway's 14,300 rolling, wooded acres also embrace thirteen lakes for swimming, fishing, boating, and waterskiing. Golfers may play sixty-three picturesque holes and sample from a recreational smorgasbord that includes tennis, skeet shooting, horsback riding, biking, and a summertime big-top circus. A half-dozen restaurants range from candlelight to casual.

Lodgings range from rooms at the Inn to deluxe villas and cottages. Callaway Gardens lies 12 scenic miles from Warm Springs and Franklin D. Roosevelt's Little White House. Contact Callaway Gardens, Pine Mountain 31822, toll-free (800) 282–8181. The Day Butterfly Center is open daily year-round. Admission of $15 per car includes all Callaway Gardens nonresort areas.

At **Pine Mountain Wild Animal Safari** (706–663–8744), you can drive your own car, or take the Safari Bus, through a 500-acre preserve populated by zebras, giraffes, camels, axis deer, gnus, antelopes, water buffalo, and other wild, nonpredatory creatures. Also visit the petting zoo, monkey house, and serpentarium, all 2 miles north of the town of Pine Mountain. Open daily 9 A.M. to dark. Adults are $10.95; senior citizens (55 and over), $9.50; ages 3 to 9, $7.50.

Blanton Creek Park, I–185 exit 11, is a nicely kept Georgia Power Company recreation area on 5,800-acre Lake Harding. The park features fifty-one RV and tent camping sites ($10 a night), which have electrical and water hookups. The park also has boat ramps, picnic pavilions, and playgrounds. Call (706) 643–7737.

A number of moderately priced motels, bed-and-breakfasts, cottages, and chalets are around Pine Mountain, Hamilton, and Warm Springs. Contact the Pine Mountain Tourism Association, P.O. Box 177, Pine Mountain 31822, (800) 441–3502.

To really get away from everything and everybody, or hang out with a gang of close friends, **Annie's Log Cabin** (706–628–5729) could be your place. Tucked among twenty wooded acres 4 miles south of Callaway Gardens, the six-room 1854 "dogtrot" log cabin sleeps as many as twelve. You'll have the entire place to yourselves, with a complete kitchen, TV, phone, a working fireplace, and a big front porch for sittin' and rockin'. Rates are $75–$95 for two persons, $10 for each additional person.

Magnolia Hall (706–628–4566), a rejuvenated Victorian cottage in the little Harris County seat of Hamilton, invites guests to stay overnight in two bedrooms and two suites furnished with antiques. A big Southern breakfast comes with the $80–$90 tariff.

Bon Cuisine Restaurant (706–663–2019), in the town of Pine Mountain north of Callaway Gardens, promises "An Adventure in Dining." It lives up to its word with a "Wild Game of the Day," which may be alligator, wild boar, antelope, snapping turtle, or white-tail deer. Tamer tastes can enjoy soft shell crab, sauteed orange roughy, filet mignon, rib-eye steak, red snapper, and flame baked shrimp. Dinner is served Monday to Saturday.

Columbus—Georgia's second largest city—will share some of the excitement of Atlanta's 1996 Summer Olympics. The Chattahoochee River city, with a metro population of about 300,000, will host Olympic softball competition, which will take place in a handsome new stadium that will be a lasting recreational legacy. Other new attractions will also be around long after the Olympians have departed. To get you bearings, stop by the **Columbus Visitor Center** (706–322–1613) at Tenth Street and Bay Avenue, facing the new Chattahoochee Riverwalk.

The ◆ **Columbus Riverwalk,** a wide brick pathway, with trees, benches, and attractive lighting, meanders a quarter-mile along the Chattahoochee in the downtown historic district. It's adorned with lots of ornamental brick and ironwork, flowers and landscaping, and steps that lead right to the river's edge. You can get out on the river, which divides Georgia from Alabama, on the ◆ *Chattahoochee Princess,* an 1850s-looking paddleboat that offers seventy-five-minute daytime cruises, romantic moonlight cruises, and evening dinner cruises. Phone (706) 324–4499 for more information.

Close to the Riverwalk, **Heritage Corner Tours,** sponsored by the Historic Columbus Foundation, takes you through four homes at the corner of Broadway and Seventh Street. They include an early 1800 pioneer log cabin; an 1828 Federal-style cottage; the Victorian cottage home of Dr. John Stith Pemberton, a Columbus pharmacist who left here for Atlanta, where he invented Coca-Cola in 1886; a mid-nineteenth-century farmhouse that now houses the Period Pieces Gift Shop; and the Victorian townhouse at 700 Broadway that serves as the Historic Foundation's headquarters. Tours begin at the headquarters for an all-inclusive $3.00. Phone (706) 322–0756 for information. If it's open—or holding one of its many regular stage productions—don't miss a chance to see the restored **Springer Opera**

29

House, built in 1871, which has hosted such illuminati as Oscar Wilde, Will Rogers, and Edwin Booth.

You can also take a walking/driving tour of numerous historic homes, churches, and public buildings with an illustrated brochure called **"Original City Tours,"** available at the Historic Columbus Foundation. **The Columbus Black Heritage** walking/driving tour takes you by churches, theaters, schools, and homes of famous Black Columbusites such as gospel and blues singer Gertrude "Ma" Rainey. Pick up a brochure at the Columbus Visitors Center.

Even if you're staunchly antiwar, don't miss the ◆**National Infantry Museum,** 101 Fourth Avenue, (706) 327–9798, on the mammoth Fort Benning Army compound. The museum's three floors and twelve spacious galleries exhibit more than 6,000 items from the French and Indian War and the Revolution, through the World Wars, and all the way to Vietnam and the Persian Gulf conflict. You'll see a porthole from the battleship *Maine,* sixteenth-century English armor, the wing of a WWII Japanese Zero, ancient Korean and Chinese weapons and armor, gas masks worn by WWI horses, and wartime documents signed by twenty U.S. presidents. It's open daily except for major national holidays. Free admission.

Also of military interest, the ◆**Confederate Naval Museum** displays the salvaged remains of the Confederate gunboats *Jackson* and *Chattahoochee.* It's open every day except Monday. Free admission.

The ◆**Columbus Museum** is a peaceful place to spend a few hours browsing. Permanent exhibits include a hands-on discovery gallery for youngsters and adults, fine arts decorative gallery, regional history gallery, and changing exhibits of regional art. Located at 1251 Wynnton Road, (706) 322–0400, the museum is open daily except Monday. Donations are invited.

If you'd like to stay in a bed-and-breakfast, the **Rothschild-Pound House,** 201 Seventh Street, Columbus 31901, (800) 585–4075, an 1870s Second Empire showplace in the historic district, has four guest suites with private baths, hot tubs, marble fireplaces, antiques, and 14-foot ceilings. Guests also enjoy an English garden and lily pond. Owners Mamie and Garry Pound include breakfast and cocktails in their $75–$125 nightly rates.

For dining in the historic district, take a table at the **Olive Branch Cafe,** 1032 Broadway, (706) 322–7410, which serves trendy continental fare, with a Greek touch to its lamb loin with spinach and olives, fried goat cheese salads, moussaka, and other specialties. **The Columbus Hilton Hotel,** on the Riverwalk, has a popular Sunday buffet brunch. The hotel, built partly in a nineteenth-century ironworks, is the city's best full-service lodging. It has an outdoor pool and bar. Doubles are $70–$120. Phone (800) 524–4020 for more information.

◆ **Providence Canyon State Park** preserves the scenic beauty of an area often referred to as "Georgia's Little Grand Canyon." More than a dozen canyons in the 1,108-acre park have been chiseled out over the past 150 years by the slow, relentless process of soil erosion. As deep as 150 feet, the canyons offer a geological primer and a stunning visual display of stratified soil layers. Many fascinating formations stand alone in the midst of the canyons.

During spring and fall, those making the easy hike to the canyon floor are rewarded by multicolored wildflowers, which complement the pinks, purples, and whites of the Providence soils. From July to September, the rare plumleaf azalea blooms in shades from light orange to salmon and various tones of red and scarlet.

Stop first at the park's interpretive center (912–838–6202) for an overview. A day-use park, Providence has picnic tables, shelters, and rest rooms. It's on Highway 39C, 7 miles west of Lumpkin, and open daily from 7:00 A.M. to dark. There is a $2.00 per visit parking fee.

You may stay overnight and fish and boat in the Chattahoochee River at ◆ **Florence Marina State Park,** Route 1, Box 36, Omaha 31821, (912) 838–6870. Campgrounds have electricity, water, rest rooms, and showers. Furnished efficiency apartments, sleeping up to five, with kitchenettes are available. Call (800) 864–PARK for rates and reservations. The park also has a swimming pool, tennis courts, a playground, and small grocery store. The park is on Highway 39C, 10 miles west of Providence Canyon. There is a $2.00 per visit parking fee.

If ◆ **Westville** were near an interstate highway, more than a million visitors a year would enjoy it. As it is, far from major thoroughfares, at the tiny Stewart County seat of Lumpkin, Georgia's "Village of the 1850s" is appreciated by only a fortunate 50,000 or so. Forty miles southeast of Columbus, 25 miles west of Jimmy Carter's Plains, this Williamsburg-style re-creation includes more than two dozen authentic nineteenth-century homes, public buildings, and craftsmen's shops lining the hard-packed clay streets.

As you walk about the town, you'll be treated to a symphony of workaday sounds: the blacksmith hammering nails, horseshoes, farm implements, and household utensils; the cobbler tapping together a pair of fine riding boots; the schoolmarm calling her charges to class. Elsewhere, townsfolk make their own soap, furniture, and candles; hand-stich quilts; and cook corn breads, stews, and gingerbread over an open hearth. A mule plods in stoic circles, turning an enormous round stone that grinds sugar cane into thick, amber syrup.

Lifestyles range from the rich and famous at the Greek Revival McDonald House to the cottages of the working folk. Every season has its special events: the Spring Festival in early April; May Pole Dances, May 1; Early American, July 4; the Fair of the 1850s, late October-early November; and, at Christmas, strolling carolers and yule log lighting.

Westville, P.O. Box 1850, Lumpkin 31815, (912) 838–6310, is open Tuesday through Saturday 10:00 A.M. to 5:00 P.M.; Sunday 1:00 to 5:00 P.M. Admission for adults is $7.00; college students and military personnel, $6.00; and ages 6–12, $3.00.

With its redbrick courthouse, granite Confederate soldier, and one-story buildings flanking the quiet square, Lumpkin could be moved, intact, into a museum as an exhibit of nineteenth-century Americana. The **Bedingfield Inn,** (912) 838–4201, was built in 1836 as a doctor's residence and stagecoach inn. It's open 1:00 to 5:00 P.M. daily.

◆ **George T. Bagby State Park,** fronting the Chatta-hoochee River's 48,000-acre Lake Walter F. George, is a resort-style getaway. The modern thirty-room Walter F. George Lodge has all the modern comforts and a full-service restaurant. Call (800) 864–PARK for lodge and cottage rates and reservations. Around it you'll find boat ramps and marinas, swimming pools, tennis courts, and hiking and picnic areas. You can also stay in furnished cottages. There's a $2.00 per visit parking fee. Contact Box 201, Ft. Gaines 31751, (912) 768–2571.

At **Frontier Village** in neighboring Ft. Gaines, authentic log cabins reflect the area's frontier heritage.

◆ **Kolomoki Mounds State Historic Park,** Route 1, Blakely 31723, (912) 723–5296, is an important archaeological site, as well as a recreation area. Within the 1,293-acre park you may climb some of the seven burial mounds and temple mounds built by Creek Indians in the twelfth and thirteenth centuries. The small museum has artifacts unearthed from the mounds and the excavated burial mound of a tribal chief. Also in the park, you're invited to swim in two pools, fish and boat in a pair of lakes, have a picnic, and play miniature golf.

The park's thirty-five camping sites have water and electricity, hot showers, and rest rooms.

Driving around the **Early County Courthouse** in Blakely, look for the monument to the peanut. A more delicious "monument" is nearby. **Miss Brown's Busy Bee Cafe,** (912) 723–3588, serves some of the best home cooking in southwest Georgia, and there's always a selection of at least a dozen pies to follow up the fried chicken, catfish, barbecue, and other hearty dishes. Lunch is served Monday through Friday.

Southern cooking's also first-rate at **Our Place,** Sawyer Shopping Center, (912) 723–8880. For trendy California-style salads, sandwiches, burgers, and entrees, try **Café on the Square,** (912) 723–8000.

Layside Bed and Breakfast, 611 River Street, Blakely 31723, (912) 723–8932, is a lovely inn in the century-old home of Jeanneane and Ted Lay. Rooms with private bath and continental breakfast are $42.18 double, $33.30 single.

If ever a body of water were created with fishermen in mind, it's got to be ❖ **Lake Seminole.** And if ever a man were created for a fisherman's lake, it must be Jack Wingate. Formed by an impoundment of the Chattahoochee and Flint Rivers, the 37,500-acre lake, with a 250-mile shoreline, is especially bountiful grounds for bass fishing. Largemouth routinely weigh in at upwards of fifteen pounds. Anglers also snare a wealth of bodacious black bass, white bass, hybrid bass, and stripers, as well as bream, chain pickerel, catfish, yellow perch, and many other varieties.

Yet the marshy, reedy lake—afloat with thousands of acres of grass beds and lily pads, and spiked with the ghostly trunks of cypress and live oak trees—is so far off the beaten path, down where Georgia's southwest corner bumps against Alabama and Florida, that when more than fifty boats appear on a single day, old-timers grumble that "Ol' Sem" is turning into a waterbound I–75.

One of the first persons you'll meet around the lake is Jack Wingate. His **Bass Island Campground and Lodge,** Route 1, Box 1571, Bainbridge 31717, (912) 246–0658, is the oldest commercial fishing camp on this whole vast waterway. Character supreme, raconteur, humorist, tall-tale teller, sometime newspaper columnist, and walking encyclopedia of anything that has to do with fishing, Wingate grew up in these parts well before the Jim Woodruff Reservoir flooded the landscape in 1957. He can point to a place, now underwater, where Spanish friars from Cuba established missions in the 1650s and another where Generals Andrew Jackson, Zachary Taylor, and Winfield Scott built a fort in 1816 to attack Seminole and Creek Indians.

With an average depth of 9 to 12 feet and in many areas shallow enough for you to stand on the bottom and flycast, these stump-studded waters can rip open an inexperienced boat like an aluminum can. Hence, you'll need the services of Wingate or one of his fellow guides ($150 a day, including fuel, boat, and motor). Some do double-duty as guides for duck hunting, for which Seminole is also renowned. You can engage them at the Lunker Lodge, off Highway 97 south, between Bainbridge and Chattahoochee, Florida.

The Lodge carries complete lines of fishing gear, ice, groceries, and rental boats. The restaurant is worth the trip, even if you're not intending to fish. Festooned with stuffed trophies, Indian arrowheads, World War I helmets, and other odds and ends, the rustic dining room specializes in absolutely first-class fried and broiled fish, shrimp, oysters, barbecue, chicken, and hearty Southern breakfasts, at very modest prices.

The adjacent Bass Island Campground and Lodge has forty-eight camp sites ($10 a night) and sixteen motel rooms with kitchenettes ($32 double). The Stag Lodge sleeps sixteen men at $6.00 each. Aspiring young fishermen between ages 8 and 14 may want to sign up for Jack Wingate's Boys Camp, a week of fishing, fun, and water sports during the summer.

The lake's other recreational area is **Seminole State Park,** off Highway 39, 16 miles south of Donalsonville (912–861–3137). Facilities include fishing, boating, swimming, waterskiing, picnicking, camping, and furnished cottages. Call (800) 864–PARK for camping and cottage rates and reservations. There is a $2.00 per visit parking fee.

PEACHES, PECANS, AND FDR

President Franklin Delano Roosevelt left his everlasting imprint on the hills and piny woodlands of Meriwether County. The future president first came to this isolated rural county, 85 miles southwest of Atlanta, in 1924 to immerse his polio-afflicted limbs in the mineral waters of Warm Springs. His ◆ **Little White House,** secluded in a wooded grove, became his sanctuary from the monumental pressures of World War II. Now maintained by the Georgia Department of Natural Resources, the comfortable little house remains as he left it when he died here on April 12, 1945.

In the kitchen, simple dishes, pots and pans, a hand-cranked ice-cream maker, and other utensils are neatly stacked. In the woodwork, FDR's cook penciled this touching message: "Daisy Bonner cook the first meal and the last one in this cottage for the President Roosevelt." The four-term president was seated in a living room chair, posing for a portrait, when he was fatally stricken. The unfinished portrait remains on its stand.

From the house, the "Walk of States" leads to the Roosevelt Museum. A twelve-minute film includes segments of home movies showing the president swimming, playing with his Scottie dog Fala, carving the Thanksgiving turkey, and driving about the countryside in his 1938 Ford convertible, equipped with hand controls. (The car, all polished, sits in the garage next to the house.) Also displayed in the museum are glass cases filled with gifts and memorabilia: his wheelchair and cigarette holder, hundreds of walking canes, and a sweater knitted by First Lady Eleanor Roosevelt.

The Little White House and Roosevelt Museum (706–655–5870) are open daily, except Thanksgiving and Christmas, 9:00 A.M. to 5:00 P.M. Admission for adults is $4.00; ages 6 to 18, $2.00; and ages 5 and under, free. Special observances on April 12 commemorate FDR's extraordinary presidency.

The adjacent village of Warm Springs (population 450) has been revived with visitors in mind. More than sixty stores along the main street are stocked with antiques, collectibles, and Georgia-made arts and crafts. The **Victorian Tea Room** (706–655–2319), a 1906 mercantile store, has been turned into a cozy dining room specializing in soups, salads, sandwiches, and Southern home cooking. It's open for lunch Tuesday through Sunday and for dinner Friday only.

The Warm Springs Welcome Center (800–FDR–1927), in the depot-looking building on the village's main street, is open every day for information and brochures. Really big appetites should check out the buffet line at **The Bulloch House** (706–655–9068), on Highway 27 just off Warm Springs's main streeet.

◆ **Franklin D. Roosevelt State Park,** about 5 miles west of Warm Springs, on Highway 190, is ideal for a minivacation. On the wooded crest of Pine Mountain, the 9,480-acre park has a lake for swimming, fishing, and boating; hiking trails; and picturesque picnic spots. Roosevelt's favorite was Dowdell's Knob, with sweeping views of the Pine Mountain Valley. Many of the fieldstone buildings in the park were the product of the Depression-era Civilian Conservation Corps. Campsites ($10 a night) have water, electricity, hot showers, and rest rooms. Cottages have fireplaces and fully equipped kitchens for standard state fees. Call (800) 864–PARK for rates and reservations. There is a $2.00 per visit parking fee. The park office, Box 749, Pine Mountain 31822, (706) 663–4858, is open daily 8:00 A.M. to 5:00 P.M.

Hikers in your crowd can lace up their boots and hit the scenic 23-mile **Pine Mountain Trail.** Starting at the Callaway Gardens Country Store on Highway 27, the trail winds past rock formations, waterfalls, big stands of trees, and lush vegetation on its way to its terminus at the TV tower on Highway 85W near Warm Springs. One of the country's southernmost mountain trails, it has twelve access points, so you can get on and off with ease. Pick up a trail map at the FDR Park office.

If you'd like to spend some time canoeing on a scenic, unspoiled river, get in touch with Jeff DeShazo at **Canoe The Flint,** 4429 Woodland Road, Thomaston 30286, (404) 647–2633. Guided and self-guided trips on the river begin at Highway 36, 15 miles south of Warm Springs. You pass through mostly mild rapids, waterfalls, hills and valleys, wildflowers, ferns, and animal habitats.

The ◆ **Pasaquan Folk Art Compound** would probably seem extraordinary even in India or the Land of Oz. In rural Marion County, near the tiny county seat of Buena Vista, this outdoor ensemble of toothy totem faces, smiling snakes, whirling pinwheels, suns, moons, and stars—all painted in brilliant primary colors—is positively otherworldly. It was the product of the late Eddie Owens Martin, who was born here in 1908, traveled to New York and abroad, and returned in 1950 to create this fabulous legacy. To finance his creativity Martin came to town in a turban and robes and told fortunes and sold jewelry around the courthouse.

Since Owens's death in 1986, his "Land of Pasaquan" has been meticulously restored and opened to the public. For information call the Marion County Chamber of Commerce at (800) 647–BVGA.

You'll find comfortable bed-and-breakfast accommodations at **Yesteryear,** a restored 1886 mansion at 229 Broad Street, Buena Vista 31803, (912) 649–7307.

Approaching Albany from any direction, you'll pass symmetrical groves of papershell pecan trees. Pecans are available year-round, still in the paper-thin shell or roasted and boxed. Some groves invite you to come in and pick your own. The attractive city of 75,000 has other pleasant surprises as well.

At ◆ **Chehaw Wild Animal Park,** on Highway 91, 2¹/₂ miles northeast of the city, (912) 430–5275, African elephants and giraffes, Andean llamas, North American black bears, bobcats, elk, bison, and deer roam in natural habitats designed by Jim Fowler, former naturalist with TV's *Wild Kingdom*. You view the animals from protected elevated walkways. Zoo admission is $2.00 for adults; senior citizens, ages 3–11, and military personnel, $1.00. An additional $2.00 a carload lets you in the companion recreational park with play areas, jogging, hiking and biking trails, a re-created Creek Indian village, miniature train rides, a boat dock, and picnic areas. The **Chehaw National Indian Festival,** held in the park the third weekend of May, is one of the Southeast Tourism Society's top twenty yearly events. The park is open 9:00 A.M. to 6:00 P.M. daily except Monday and Christmas.

Thronateeska Heritage Foundation, 100 Roosevelt Avenue, (912) 432–6955, is a delightful time-trip through the nineteenth and early twentieth centuries. The complex includes an early 1900s "prairie style" train depot, a 1910 steam locomotive, an 1840s house, and a planetarium and science center in a vintage Railway Express Co. office. It's open Monday to Friday from noon to 5:00 P.M., Sunday from 2:00 to 5:00 P.M.

The **Albany Museum of Art,** 311 Meadowlark Drive, (912)

37

439–8400, has permanent and changing displays of regional and national artists. Open Tuesday to Saturday from 10:00 A.M. to 5:00 P.M., Sunday from 2:00 to 5:00 P.M. Admission for adults is $2.00; students, $1.00; under 12, no charge.

Carr's Steak House, 609 North Slappey Drive, (912) 439–8788, is a favorite place for steaks, seafoods, cocktails, and dancing. Lunch and dinner are served Monday through Saturday. Albanians also enjoy the dining room of the **Quality Inn Merry Acres,** 1504 Dawson Road, (912) 439–2261.

Contact the Albany Chamber of Commerce, Box 308, Albany 31702, (912) 883–6900.

Every spring in the swamps and bogs of southwest Georgia, a throny, scrubby, rather homely tree called the mayhaw produces an applelike fruit prized by gourmets and homemakers. The small, coral-hued fruit is gathered in fishing nets and by hand, and then turned into a delectable sweet-tart jelly that's sold in stores around the small Miller County seat of Colquitt. The fruit is the star of Colquitt's early April Mayhaw Festival.

While you're in the Colquitt area, try to catch a performance of ❖ **"Swamp Gravy,"** an entertaining folklife play about the comedies and tragedies, tall tales, music, dance, and songs of Miller County and rural Georgia. Sponsored by the Colquitt/Miller Arts Council, it's performed in March, April, October, and November. Call (912) 758–5450 for more information.

The Tarrer Inn, 155 South Cuthbert Street, Colquitt 31737, (912) 758–2888, is another welcome newcomer to downtown Colquitt. Built in 1861 as a boardinghouse, the Inn has recently been refurbished as a comfortable small hotel. Twelve guest rooms are decorated with antiques and modern amenities. Your continental breakfast comes with biscuits and homemade mayhaw jelly. At lunch and dinner the restaurant is renowned for its yeast rolls and fried chicken. Rates are $62.50 to $89.00.

You can hardly miss **The John Dill House,** 102 South Washington Street, Fort Gaines 31751, (912) 768–2338, as you drive through tiny Fort Gaines. The two-story house is painted brilliant pink, which innkeepers Ramona and Philip Kurland say was the original shade when the house was built in the late 1820s. The Kurlands have nine guest bedrooms, with many pieces of Victoriana. Each room has a private bath, and the Kurlands will send you off with a hearty breakfast. Rates are $65 for a double. You may also enjoy browsing the gift shop.

If you're a fan of country fairs and enjoy good, old-fashioned fun, put ❖ **Climax Swine Time** (912–246–0910) on your post-Thanksgiving calendar. Held the Friday and Saturday after Thanksgiving, in the Decatur County community of Climax, many of the activities are pig-related: a hog-calling contest, best-dressed pig competition, a greased-pig chase, and a "chitlin" (chitterling) eating contest. Also on the agenda are country and gospel music, a 10-K race, cane grinding and syrup making, and barbecue and fried chicken for those who care not for "chitlins."

The ❖ **Rattlesnake Roundup** (912–762–4243), the last weekend of January, is the social event of the year at the small Grady County town of Whigham, 6 miles east of Climax. The event began a couple of decades ago when Whigham residents, tired of being accosted by the hissing reptiles every time they walked through their fields and farms, decided to do something about it and have some sport at the same time. On the big day, visitors pack tiny downtown Whigham as snakes by the hundreds are brought in and displayed.

CARTER COUNTRY

Peach County leaves little doubt that it's the heart of Georgia's most luscious industry. Traveling on I–75 at night, you can't miss "The Big Peach," an enormous illuminated rendition of the fruit on a hundred-foot-pole at the Byron/Fort Valley exit. During the summer, visitors have plenty of opportunities to go into the orchards and pick their own or to buy fresh peaches at packing houses and roadside stands. The Byron/Fort Valley exit 49 is the northern end of the Andersonville Trail, which leads through Fort Valley to Plains on Highways 49 and 280.

In mid-June you're invited to the **Georgia Peach Festival** in Byron and Fort Valley. This weeklong event includes parades, street dances, peach pie cookoffs, peach-eating contests, and a king-and-queen coronation.

Six miles south of Fort Valley, at the Peach/Macon County line, look for a left turn off Highway 49 into Massee Lane Gardens, home of the ❖ **American Camellia Society.** Between November and March, pink and white blossoms in every known variety bloom in the Society's nine-acre gardens. All year round, you're invited into the Society's Williamsburg-style headquarters to admire the 170 porcelain birds and flowers created in the studios of the late American artist, Edward Marshall Boehm. The pieces are so lifelike they appear to be on the verge of flight. Some were created as gifts-of-state from presidents and kings.

The American Camellia Society, P.O. Box 1217, Fort Valley 31030, (912) 967–2358, has open grounds daily from dawn to dusk; the headquarters building and Boehm collection are open Monday through Friday 8:30 A.M. to 4:00 P.M.

Part of the Andersonville Trail, Macon County is the home of Georgia's largest Mennonite community. You may admire antebellum white columns in the small towns of Marshallville and Montezuma.

The Macon County seat and a thriving Mennonite Community, ◆ **Montezuma** was named by returning Mexican War veterans—which accounts for the Aztec Loan Co., Aztec Motel, and other enterprises. Nearly one hundred Mennonite families give the little town some of the appearance of the Pennsylvania Dutch country. Drive east of Montezuma on Highway 26 past the neat barns and silos and the contented herds of the Mennonite dairy farms. Three miles from Montezuma—and 14 miles west of I–75 exit 41—look for a black buggy parked in front of **Yoder's Deitsch Haus** (912–472–2024), a sparkling clean cafeteria where Mennonites in traditional dress prepare truly admirable Southern cooking, spiced with such Pennsylvania Dutch specialties as shoofly pie and pot roast. Before leaving, stop by the bakery for a sackful of cakes, cookies, breads, and strudel. It's open for breakfast, lunch, and dinner Tuesday through Saturday. Handmade Mennonite dolls, afghans, coverlets, garden ornaments, and other items are on sale in the adjacent gift shop.

You may pick up a driving tour map from the Macon County Chamber of Commerce, P.O. Box 308, Montezuma 31063, (912) 472–2391.

Sumter County, the epicenter of Georgia's peanut industry, is home of the world's most famous peanut farmer, our thirty-ninth president. The southern anchor of the Andersonville Trail, Sumter is also the site of the Civil War's most notorious prisoner-of- war camp.

These days, all is green and peaceful at the ◆ **Andersonville National Cemetery and Historic Site.** Stop first at the National Park Service Visitors Center to view the film and exhibits, then take the self-guided driving tour.

Built in 1864 as confinement for 10,000 Union prisoners of

war, the 26½-acre stockade soon became a charnel house for upwards of 33,000 captives. With the Confederacy barely able to feed and clothe its own forces, about 12,000 of the Andersonville inmates perished of disease and starvation. As park rangers point out, however, Southern prisoners in the more well-off North often fared no better than the Union prisoners at Andersonville.

After the war, the camp commander, Swiss-born Captain Henry Wirz, was found guilty of war crimes and hanged. The self-guided tour leads you past thousands of graves and impressive memorials erected by states whose sons died here. Tunnels testify to the prisoners' usually failed attempts to escape the horrors.

Portions of the massive log stockade have recently been reconstructed to give visitors a better idea of the conditions that existed here. A new **Prisoner of War Museum** honors Americans taken captive in all our wars, including the Persian Gulf War.

A granite springhouse marks the site of **Providence Spring**, which legends says flowed from barren ground in answer to prisoners' prayers.

Across Highway 49, the village of **Andersonville** (population 250) has been returned to its 1860s appearance. At the Train Depot–Welcome Center, you'll be greeted by Peggy Sheppard, a live-wire transplanted from Yonkers, New York. She'll direct you to the village's antiques and craft shops, picnic groves, and antebellum churches and homes. The **Drummer Boy Museum** houses an extensive collection of guns, swords, battle flags, and documents signed by Jefferson Davis and Abraham Lincoln. The village's major yearly happenings are **Andersonville Antiques and Civil War Artifacts Fair** in early May and **Andersonville Historic Fair** in early October, which features battle reenactments and scores of craftsmen and musicians.

Andersonville National Historic Site (912–924–0343), Andersonville 31711, is open daily 8:00 A.M. to 5:00 P.M. Also contact Andersonville Town Council (912–924–2558) at the same address.

Peggy Sheppard runs a charming country bed-and-breakfast called **"A Place Away."** The two bedrooms in the comfortable, rustic-looking cottage have private baths, working fireplaces, refrigerators, and coffeemakers. Guest rooms and a sitting room are decorated in kick-off-your-shoes casual country style. Rates of $50 double come with a bountiful Southern breakfast. Contact Andersonville Welcome Center, Andersonville 31711, (912) 924–2558.

At nearby **Americus,** stop at the Americus/Sumter County Chamber of Commerce on 400 West Lamar Street, (912) 924–2646, for a driving guide to the historic showplaces around the pleasant city of 20,000. Memorabilia of our thirty-ninth president are displayed at the **James Earl Carter Library** of Georgia Southwestern College.

For contemporary comforts wrapped in a splendid turn-of-the-century package, check into the ◆ **Windsor Hotel** in downtown Americus. Built in 1896, the redbrick, turreted-and-towered Italianate landmark reopened in 1991 to rave reviews. The fifty-three large guest rooms ($65 double) are beautifully furnished and decorated. The Grand Dining Room serves high-Southern and continental cuisine, and there's a full bar and an open veranda with wicker rockers. The private Lindbergh Dining Room was named for "Lucky Lindy," who purchased his first plane and made his first solo flight from nearby Souther Field. Some old-timers remember him playing pool across the street from the hotel. The Windsor is at 104 Windsor Avenue, Americus 31709. Call (912) 924–1555 or toll-free (800) 252–7466.

At the **DeSoto Confectionery & Nut Co.,** 13 miles east of Americus on Highway 280, the area's renowned product is sold in and out of the shell; wrapped in vanilla, chocolate, and peanut butter fudge; and peanut brittled, caramelized with corn, and otherwise glorified. The "Nut House" is open Monday through Saturday. They also do a booming mail-order business. Write P.O. Box 72, DeSoto 31743, or call (912) 874–1200.

More than a dozen years after leaving the White House, Jimmy Carter is still a magnet for visitors to his little hometown of **Plains.** Stop first at the Plains Visitors Center, on Highway 280 between Plains and Americus, to pick up information on attractions all over the area. The center also has its own stocked fishing pond. In town go first to the National Park Service Visitors Center in the former train depot/presidential campaign headquarters to see displays and hundreds of photos of the Carters.

Most of the landmarks associated with Carter's before-during-and-after presidency are included in the ◆ **Jimmy Carter National Historic Site.** One of the best ways to see them is on a guided tour. **B.J.'s Tours,** which depart from B.J.'s Pit Stop (formerly Brother Billy's service station), take you by Plains

High School, Carter's family farm and boyhood home, and the ranch-style home where he now lives. The cost is modest, and tours are laced with plenty of humorous anecdotes. When the former president is in town, he often appears at local social functions. On Sundays he teaches a class at Maranatha Baptist Church.

Shops on the 1-block Main Street are stocked with Carter paraphernalia and, naturally, peanuts in many different guises.

Plains Bed and Breakfast, in the Victorian house where Carter's parents spent their early married years, has antique furnishings and modern comforts, but no souvenirs of the famous parents' boarding days. Doubles with private bath and full breakfast cost $50. Write Plains Bed and Breakfast, P.O. Box 217, Plains 31780, or call (912) 824–7252. Also contact Jimmy Carter National Historic Site, Plains 31780, (912) 824–3413.

◆ **Georgia Veterans Memorial State Park** is a tranquil haven 9 miles west of Cordele and the racetrack lanes of I–75. A museum and vintage aircraft honor the state's military veterans. The park sits on Lake Blackshear, an 18-mile-long waterway renowned for catfish, black bass, bream, pickerel, and other delicious catches. Visitors may also enjoy boating, an eighteen-hole golf course, swimming in a freshwater pool, and a nature interpretive center and playground. The one hundred camping and trailer sites have electricity, water, rest rooms, and hot showers. Ten two- and three-bedroom cottages, with fireplaces and fully equipped kitchens, are available. For rates and reservations call (800) 864–PARK. There is a $2.00 per visit parking fee. The park office, on Highway 280, Cordele 31015, (912) 273–2190, is open daily 8:00 A.M. to 5:00 P.M.

Daphne Lodge, on Highway 280 near the park entrance, (912) 273–2596, is a pleasantly rustic, family-owned restaurant famous for its fried catfish and hushpuppies. They also serve shrimp, steaks, and fried chicken at dinner Tuesday through Saturday.

If you're down this way the first week of July, join in the fun of Cordele's annual **Watermelon Festival.**

ROSES AND PINE TREES

The ◆ **Georgia Agrirama** is an off-the-beaten-path experience less than a quarter-mile off the well-beaten paths of I–75.

43

About three dozen vintage farm buildings make up the state's agricultural heritage center. Inside the gates of this nineteenth-century time warp, youngsters may go nose-to-nose with friendly farmyard animals and take a trip on a steam-powered logging train. Cotton is planted in the old-fashioned way by a farmer in bib overalls commanding a mule and a plow. The village blacksmith hammers out nails and utensils over a white-hot forge. Sugar cane is harvested by hand and ground into syrup and corn into grits and meal at a picture-postcard gristmill. A country store sells handmade quilts, preserves, cookbooks, toys, and corn shuck dolls. On Saturday nights between mid-April and mid-October, **"The Wiregrass Opry"** is a gala open-air revue with clog dancers, bluegrass fiddlers, and gospel singers.

The Agrirama, P.O. Box Q, Tifton 31793, (912) 386-3344, is open from Labor Day through May 31, Monday through Saturday 9:00 A.M. to 5:00 P.M. and Sunday 12:30 to 5:00 P.M.; June 1 to Labor Day, daily 9:00 A.M. to 6:00 P.M. All-inclusive admission is $6.00 adults; $5.00 ages 55 and over; $3.00 ages 4 to 16; no charge, under 4. "Wiregrass Opry" is $4.00 per car.

From 1870 to the turn of the new century, Thomasville was a Southern Newport, the forefather of Palm Beach and Miami. Encouraged by reports of the area's healthy climate, wealthy Northerners came by private train to spend the winter at grand hotels, which brought chefs and orchestras all the way from New York and Europe. Many regular visitors built their own lavish homes and purchased surrounding plantations for grouse and quail hunting. In the early 1900s, the rich and famous discovered Florida, and Thomasville's "Golden Age" was over. Left behind was a remarkable heritage. Presidents, aristocrats, and "commoners" still flock to the city of 20,000 to hunt game birds and antiques, tour homes and plantations, and participate in late April's Thomasville Rose Festival.

Stop first at the Destination Thomasville Tourism Authority Welcome Center, 109 South Broad Street, (912) 225-3919 and (800) 704-2350, where you can load up on maps, brochures, and self-guided walking and driving tour information. Guides can be arranged for tour groups. The Welcome Center is open Monday to Friday 9:00 A.M. to 5:00 P.M. and Saturday 10:00 A.M. to 3:00 P.M.

On your own, stop at the **Thomas County Historical Museum,** 725 North Dawson Street, where you'll see hundreds of photos and souvenirs of the "Golden Age." It's open daily 2:00 to 5:00 P.M. Admission for adults is $4.00; students, $1.00.

Nearby, the ❖ **Lapham-Patterson House,** 626 North Dawson Street, (912) 225–4004, is an outlandish Victorian mansion built for Chicago shoe manufacturer C. W. Lapham. Maintained as a state historical museum, the tri-winged, mustard-yellow mansion is highlighted by cantilevered interior balconies, double-flue chimneys, and fish-scale shingles. It's open Tuesday through Saturday 9:00 A.M. to 5:00 P.M.; Sunday 2:00 to 5:00 P.M. Admission is charged: adults, $3.00; ages 6–18, $1.00; under age 5, free

❖ **Pebble Hill Plantation** (912–226–2344) is a "must-see." The twenty-eight-room Georgian and Greek Revival main house and the gardens, stables, and kennels were left as a museum by the late Pansy Ireland Poe. Inside the house are thirty-three original John James Audubon bird prints and extensive collections of silver, crystal, and antique furnishings. Five miles southwest of Thomasville, on Highway 319, it's open Tuesday through Saturday 10:00 A.M. to 5:00 P.M. and Sunday 1:00 to 5:00 P.M. Adult admission fee is $2.00 grounds, $5.00 main house; under age 6 not permitted in main house.

Susina Plantation Inn, Route 3, Box 1010, Thomasville 31792, (912) 377–9644, is your doorway to Old South romance. In this white-columned Greek Revival masterpiece, rooms are furnished with canopy beds, antiques, and all the contemporary conveniences. Rates of $150 a couple per night, $100 single, include a Southern hunt breakfast and a candlelight dinner with wine. You can unwind at the swimming pool and lighted tennis court.

Several of Thomasville's most beautiful old homes welcome bed-and-breakfast guests. All take pride in their antique furnishings and traditional south Georgia hospitality.

Some of the nicest homes include the **1884 Paxton House,** 445 Remington Avenue, (800) 278–0138; **Evans House,** 725 South Hansell Street, (800) 344–4717; **Grand Victoria Inn,** 817 South Hansell Street, (912) 226–7460; **Our Cottage on the Park,** 801 South Hansell Street, (912) 227–0404; and **Serendipity Cottage,** 339 East Jefferson Street, (912) 226–8111. Most are in the $65–$100 price range and include breakfast. The zip code is 31792.

The city has several good restaurants. **The Grand Old House** is that and then some. In a white-columned neo-classical mansion at 502 South Broad Street, (912) 277–0108, you'll be treated to such elegant dishes as scampi Madagascar, seafood gumbo,

45

lobster bisque, crabcakes, duck, quail, lamb, beef, and seafood. Wine and cocktails are available. Lunch and dinner are served Monday through Saturday. **The Tavern,** downstairs, serves drinks and more casual pub and bistro food and live music on weekends.

Melissa's, in a cleverly redone laundry warehouse at 134 South Madison Street, (912) 228–9844, does beer-battered shrimp, chicken tarragon salad, black bean cakes, pastas, and grilled double-cut pork chops. Lunch and dinner are served Monday through Saturday.

Other established local favorites include **Mom & Dad's Italian Restaurant,** 1800 Smith Avenue, (912) 226–6265; **The Plaza,** with Greek and American fare, 217 South Broad Street, (912) 226–5153; and **Fallin's Real Pit Bar-B-Que,** 2250 East Pinetree Boulevard, (912) 228–1071.

If you'd like to enjoy a bit of Thomasville's sporting life, shoot some skeet, and hunt birds and game, contact **Foxfire Hunting Preserve,** P.O. Box 26, Thomasville 31799, (800) 666–4899, and **Myrtlewood Plantation,** P.O. Box 32, Thomasville 31799, (912) 228–6232.

Apafia Farm, Route 2, Box 92–D, Hansell Chastain Road, Thomasville 31792, (912) 228–1682, offers Western-style horseback rides through plantation country.

Thomasville's really big annual event is the late April **Rose Festival,** a week of parades, pageantry, home tours, and rose judgings that attracts visitors from many countries. In the good-news-bad-news category, the renowned Thomasville Rose Test Garden has closed, but it's been replaced by the ❖ **Thomasville Rose Garden,** which displays scores of varieties of blooming plants around the shores of Cherokee Lake, at the corner of Covington and Smith Avenues. Admission is free.

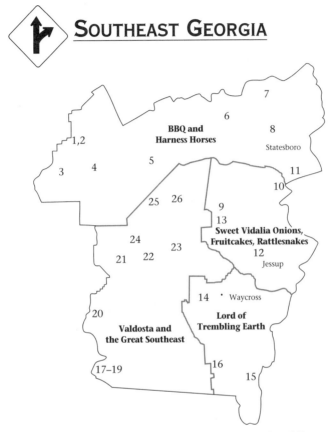

SOUTHEAST GEORGIA

BBQ and
Harness Horses

Statesboro

Sweet Vidalia Onions,
Fruitcakes, Rattlesnakes

Jessup

Waycross

Lord of
Trembling Earth

Valdosta and
the Great Southeast

1. New Perry Hotel
2. Museum of Aviation
3. Big Pig Jig
4. Harness Racing Festival
5. Bellevue Avenue
6. George L. Smith State Park
7. Magnolia Springs State Park
8. Statesboro/University
   Museum
9. Vidalia Sweet Onion
10. Fruitcake Plant Tours
11. Rattlesnake Roundup
12. Lake Grace
13. Edwin L. Hatch Nuclear Plant
    Visitors Center
14. Okefenokee Swamp Park/
    Laura S. Walker State Park

15. Suwannee Canal Recreation
    Area
16. Stephen C. Foster State Park
17. Valdosta
18. The Crescent
19. Hahira Honeybee Festival
20. Reed Bingham State Park
21. Jefferson Davis Memorial
    Museum/Crystal Lake Water
    Park
22. General Coffee State Park
23. Douglas's public golf courses
24. Blue and Gray Museum
25. Statue of Liberty
26. Little Ocmulgee State Park

Southeast Georgia

BBQ and Harness Horses

The ◆ **New Perry Hotel** has been a beacon for middle Georgia travelers since the 1920s, when it replaced a circa 1854 country inn. In bygone days, when Highway 41 funneled Florida-bound vacationers through the center of Perry, the New Perry's cheerful guest rooms—and especially its dining room—were a command performance. Even now, with most of the traffic a mile away on I-75, weary motorists still find their way to this surviving vestige of small-town hospitality.

Set among trees and gardens, across from the Houston (*Houseton*) County Courthouse, the New Perry has thirty-seven rooms in its main building and seventeen more in a modern motel-type addition by the swimming pool. They go for a modest $35–$48 a night. They're nice, comfortable, and air-conditioned, but the dining room is the main attraction.

With its starched white tablecloths, fresh flowers, bird and floral prints, this is the genteel Southern dining room personified. The menu is the chapter-and-verse Sunday Southern dinner: fried chicken, broiled Spanish mackerel and perch, baked ham, turkey and dressing, stewed corn, turnip greens, yams, green beans, congealed salads, shrimp cocktail, pecan and peach pies. Breakfast is also the full Southern board of grits, hot biscuits, sausage, ham, and eggs.

Breakfast, lunch, and dinner are served daily, at prices that are inexpensive by any standard. Breakfast will be about $4.50, lunch around $6.00, and dinner with entree, three vegetables, and chilled relish tray, less than $10.00. No alcohol is served. Contact the New Perry at 800 Main Street, Perry 31069, (912) 987–1000.

Swift Street Inn, 1204 Swift Street, Perry 31069, (912) 988–4477, is a gem of a bed-and-breakfast. Four guest rooms in the 1850s raised cottage are furnished with antiques and modern baths. A bountiful Southern breakfast comes with the $65–$85 tariff.

The ◆ **Museum of Aviation,** 2 miles south of Warner Robins Air Force Base, is a tribute to our winged military might. In two huge buildings you can admire more than seventy-five American and foreign military aircraft. You can also see a film on the history of the Air Force and numerous exhibits and displays.

Take I–75 exit 45 (Centerville/Warner Robins) and follow the signs through the city of Warner Robins. Open daily 10:00 A.M. to 5:00 P.M. Free admission. Telephone (912) 926–6870.

After touring the Aviation Museum, tuck into a big plate of spicy middle-Georgia-style barbecue draped in rich, red sauce, with sides of cole slaw, corn bread, and fried corn at **Pomos House of Barbecue,** 2766 Watson Boulevard, Warner Robins, (912) 953–2060.

Barbecue is dear to Georgians' hearts, celebrated in song and story, and exalted at annual festivals such as the ❖ **Big Pig Jig** the second weekend of October at the little middle-Georgia town of Vienna (*Vie-enna*). Dubbed the "Cadillac of Barbecue Contests" and proclaimed the state of Georgia's official barbecue cooking contest by the state legislature, this is serious business indeed. The winning team takes home prize money, trophies, bragging rights, and the honor of representing Georgia at the annual International Pig Cook-off at Memphis, Tennessee— and just maybe coming back as world champion of the barbecuing arts.

Of course, there's a fun side to all this serious business. Judges sample the secret sauces, which, according to the rules, may include "any nonpoisonous substances" and the flavors and textures of ribs, shoulders, and other succulent portions of the porkers. Famished festivalgoers also get their chance to savor the entries and take part in a host of other activities. There's always plenty of bluegrass and country music, square dancing and clog dancing, arts and crafts, a 5-kilometer "Hog Jog," and a "Whole Hog Parade," featuring handsome porkers, still not ready for the grill, decked out in all manner of zany costumes.

For information contact Dooly County Chamber of Commerce, 204-A West Union Street, Vienna 31092, (912) 268–4500.

Hawkinsville, the Pulaski County seat, is Georgia's harness racing capital. The ❖ **Harness Racing Festival,** the first weekend of April, celebrates this sport, which has been a part of Pulaski County's life since the late 1800s, when the county's mild climate made it a popular winter training grounds for harness horses from the Midwest, the Northeast, and Canada.

Nowadays, more than 350 of the sleek, high-stepping trotters and pacers come to the town of 4,000 between October and April. On the two-day festival weekend, more than 10,000 spectators crowd the grandstand at the festival grounds to watch the

49

races and enjoy the country fair atmosphere that surrounds the red clay track. For those not familiar with the sport, the horses have two decidedly different gaits. Pacers wear plastic leg hoops (called hobbles) that cause the legs on each side of their body to move in tandem: left front and left rear, right front and right rear. Trotters navigate with a diagonal gait: left front and right rear legs move together, likewise right front and left rear. They seem to effortlessly pull the colorfully silked jockeys riding behind them in light two-wheeled sulkies.

After the festival the horses pack up and head for the big-money tracks up north. One thing missing from the event is parimutuel betting. Georgia law prohibits it, but that doesn't mean you can't find some friendly unofficial wagers around the track.

Away from the track, Hawkinsville's main attractions are its restored turn-of-the-century opera house and Georgia's only major kiwifruit farm. Built in early 1907 as a stop on the vaudeville circuit between New York and New Orleans, the **Old Opera House** was abandoned in the 1950s and was about to fall totally into ruins when a group of Pulaski County businesspeople came to its rescue a few years ago. Now it hosts touring concerts and local productions. If you're here when an event is scheduled, come and spend a nostalgic evening in the restored horseshoe-shaped auditorium.

Double Q Farms, (912) 892–3794, 8 miles from town, is Janis and Charles Quimby's kiwi "ranch." There they raise the delicious green fruit with the fuzzy brown skin that most of us associate with New Zealand. When the kiwis reach their peak in October, you can go out onto the seven-acre farm and pick your own. Janis Quimby's kiwi jams and jellies are sold at the farm store and shipped around the world. Kiwi jalapeño jelly is a big favorite.

The Black Swan Inn, 411 Progress Avenue, Hawkinsville 31036, (912) 783–4466, a white-columned early-twentieth-century Southern Colonial mansion, is Hawkinsville's premier lodging. It was named for *The Black Swan,* a nineteenth-century paddlewheel steamboat that carried cargo and passengers up the Ocmulgee River that runs through downtown Hawkinsville. The inn's six guest rooms have private baths and period furnishings. A suite has a whirlpool tub. Rates of $50–$70 include a light continental breakfast. The inn's dining room offers traditional Southern cooking with pastas, steak with mushrooms and bearnaise sauces, duck, veal, fish and chicken dishes, cheesecakes, and European-style desserts.

Several antiques shops are on Broad Street, Hawkinsville's main street. For other information call **Hawkinsville-Pulaski County Chamber of Commerce,** P.O. 561, Hawkinsville 31036, (912) 783–1717.

That wonderful but sadly fading American landmark, the small-town cafe, is alive and well in Dublin. **Ma Hawkins Cafe,** near the Laurens County Courthouse at 124 West Jackson Street, (912) 272–0941, has been a citadel of Southern home cooking since 1931. Now operated by a grandson of the foundress, the cheerful cafe specializes in Southern-style breakfast—if you've been timid about sampling grits, Ma Hawkins is the place—and lunch and dinner plates highlighted by corn bread, chicken and dumplings, fried chicken, slowly simmered turnip greens and other fresh vegetables, and homemade desserts.

The cafe's front table is the traditional forum for Dublin's movers and shakers, who congregate throughout the day to jaw about the weather, crops, football, politics, and the general flow of life. The cafe is open for breakfast, lunch, and dinner Monday through Saturday. No credit cards are accepted, but it's hard to spend more than $5.00.

If you'd like to try your own hand at corn bread, using the absolutely freshest possible ingredients, head for **Chappell's Mill** (912–272–5128), Highway 441, 13 miles north of Dublin. Built in 1811 and saved from destruction by General William T. Sherman's Union army, the old mill grinds about 15,000 bushels of corn a year into the right stuff for light, golden corn bread. Watch it ground, then buy a two-pound bag for 60 cents, five pounds for $1.10. Call before visiting.

Dublin's nineteenth-century Irish heritage is reflected in its annual **St. Patrick's Day Festival,** a lively round of parades, beauty pageants, arts and crafts, square dancing, softball, and golf tournaments. Along the emerald green lawns of the city's ◆ **Bellevue Avenue,** many photogenic Greek Revival and Victorian showplaces parade the year-round.

◆ **George L. Smith State Park,** off Highway 23, 4 miles southeast of Twin City, is a quiet, lightly used retreat with twenty-one fully equipped camping sites, picnic areas, and a fishing lake with rental boats. Write P.O. Box 57, Twin City 30471, or call (912) 763–2759 or (800) 864–PARK for camping reservations. Two very nice bed-and-breakfasts are in the Emanuel County seat of Swainsboro: **Coleman House,** 323 North Main Street, (912) 237–2822, and **Edenfield House Inn,** 358 Church Street, (912) 237–3007. Both are in zip code 30401.

◆ **Magnolia Springs State Park,** Highway 25, 5 miles north of Millen, is one of the prettiest and quietest in the whole park system. Huge old trees bend their limbs over clear springs flowing at an estimated nine million gallons a day. It's a lovely spot to spread a picnic. You can also swim, dabble your bait for fish, and walk along nature trails. You may even want to camp out overnight or stay in a furnished cottage. There is a $2.00 per visit parking fee. Contact Magnolia Springs State Park, Route 5, Box 488, Millen 30442, (912) 982–1660 or (800) 864–PARK for camping and cottage reservations.

Adjoining the park, the **Bo Ginn National Fish Hatchery and Aquarium,** (912) 982–1700, has twenty-six tanks showing off the fish raised at the hatchery.

Tree-shaded ◆ **Statesboro** (population 21,000) is the Bulloch County seat and home of 14,000 Georgia Southern University students. The ◆ **University Museum,** (912) 681–5444, has a fascinating collection of dinosaur fossils, do-touch exhibits, and revolving scientific and technological displays. The "star" attraction is **The Plant Votgle Whale,** a 45-million-year-old leviathan that scientists believe walked on sturdy legs. It was discovered at Georgia Power Company's Plant Votgle in neighboring Burke County.

Near the campus, the ten-acre **Botanical Gardens** grow around a restored nineteenth-century farmhouse and outbuildings. After trekking around the gardens, bring your best boardinghouse reach to the **Beaver House,** 121 South Main Street, (912) 764–2821. The dining room table groans under a delicious family-style buffet that includes fried chicken, fish, baked ham, roast beef, and numerous vegetables, relishes, and desserts. It's open daily except Saturday for lunch ($6.49) and dinner ($6.99). **Vandy's Barbecue,** downtown at 22 Vine Street, (912) 764–2444, is another culinary landmark.

The **Statesboro Inn,** 106 South Main Street, (912) 489–8628, serves refined American and continental dishes. Double rooms with antiques and modern baths are $65, including full Southern breakfast.

Statesboro is a short drive off I–16, 60 miles west of Savannah. Contact Convention and Visitors Bureau, 332 South Main Street, Statesboro 30460, (800) 568–3301.

SWEET VIDALIA ONIONS, FRUITCAKES,

RATTLESNAKES

The sandy soil of Toombs, Treutlen, and neighboring southeast Georgia counties yields a favorite gourmet delicacy. The well-known ◆ **Vidalia Sweet Onion** takes its name from the Toombs County town of Vidalia. During the summer, you can buy 'em by the sackful or carload at roadside stands in and around the town of 10,000.

The **Robert Toombs Inn** in downtown Lyons (5 miles east of Vidalia) is a modern pairing of two early 1900s hotels. Fourteen single rooms and five small suites have modern baths and Early American furnishings: rates range from $48–$55. The dining room features Tex-Mex food. The full bar is a rarity in a small Georgia town. The inn is at 101 South State Street, Lyons 30436; call (912) 526–4489.

Claxton, seat of Evans County, is famous for fruitcakes and rattlesnakes. As you drive into the small town, you're very nearly intoxicated by the sweet aroma of baking fruitcakes. More than 6 million pounds of the holiday treats are produced annually in Claxton's modern bakeries. You can get information on ◆ **Fruitcake Plant Tours** and other area attractions at the Claxton Welcome Center, 4 North Duval Street, Claxton 30417, (912) 739–2281.

If you're here in mid-March, you can take part in the festivities surrounding the annual ◆ **Rattlesnake Roundup.** Begun, simply, in 1968 as an effort to reduce the venomous reptile's threat to man and beast, the roundup has grown into a major happening, with a parade, hundreds of arts and crafts booths, home cooking, and such rattler-related events as awards for the most snakes brought in, the longest, the fattest, and so on. A reptile expert "milks" the snakes of their deadly venom, which is used in antivenom serums and other medicines.

In neighboring Tattnall County, **Gordonia-Altamaha State Park,** P.O. Box 1047, Reidsville 30453, (912) 557–6444, has twenty-five tent and trailer sites with water and electricity, hot showers, and rest rooms as well as a swimming pool, boat dock, and plenty of good fishing places. There's also a new nine-hole golf course. Call (800) 864–PARK for camping reservations.

If you're a fishing family, you may come close to nirvana in Wayne County. One county removed from the Atlantic Coast, Wayne includes 60 miles of the **Altamaha River,** a waterway rich with several varieties of bass, bream, perch, and catfish. ◆ **Lake Grace,** on Highway 301 near the Wayne County seat of Jesup, is a local favorite. The 250 acres include plenty of secluded fishing spots, as well as opportunities for boating, swimming, waterskiing, picnics, and camping. Contact the park superintendent at (912) 579–6475.

Pine Lake (912–427–3664), near the small community of Gardi, features a stocked twenty-acre lake tailored for bank fishing. You may also enjoy a swimming pool, shaded picnic areas, and campsites with electricity, water, and rest rooms.

Jaycee Landing (912–427–7987), on Highway 301 north, has a number of boat ramps in the Altamaha, as well as a general store with food and all your favorite kinds of fishing bait. Campsites have water, electricity, rest rooms, and showers.

Your camaraderie with local anglers is bound to lead you to some especially rewarding, off-the-beaten path fishing spots!

When you've bagged your limit, enjoy a large sample of Southeast Georgia cooking at **Jones' Kitchen,** on Main Street in Jesup, (912) 427–4100. The all-you-can-eat daily luncheon spread includes fresh local fish, chicken, meat loaf, vegetables, several kinds of salads, and a peach or apple cobbler for less than you'd pay for lunch at a fast-food outlet.

Jesup, an industrious town of 10,000, has a number of beautifully maintained Victorian homes, which you can drive past with a brochure provided by the Wayne County Chamber of Commerce, P.O. Box 70, Jesup 31545, (912) 427–2028.

The ◆ **Edwin L. Hatch Nuclear Plant Visitors Center,** on U.S. Highway 1, 14 miles north of Baxley, will tell you all you ever wanted to know about this controversial source of energy. The story is told with films, hands-on exhibits, and animated displays. Open Monday to Friday 9:00 A.M. to 5:00 P.M. and Sunday 1:00 to 5:00 P.M. Phone (912) 367–3668.

You can unwind at **Lake Mayers,** a locally popular resort with fishing, boating, swimming, waterskiing, and picnic areas. Lake Mayers is off U.S. Highway 341, 8 miles west of Baxley.

Nonmembers may play the Appling Country Club's 9-hole golf course. Phone (912) 367–3582.

LAND OF TREMBLING EARTH

◆ **Okefenokee Swamp Park,** off Highway 1, 8 miles south of Waycross, is the most popular of three entrances to the vast, mysterious "Land of Trembling Earth." Although most of the park is actually outside the boundaries of the 700-square-mile, 412,000-acre Okefenokee National Wildlife Refuge, guided boat tours and cypress boardwalks lead you well into this fascinating world.

The Swamp Park is the most casual visitor-oriented of the three entrances—the others are in neighboring Charlton County—with numerous exhibits, interpretive centers, wildlife shows, and other visual displays.

Stop first at the cedar-roofed welcome center adjacent to the paved parking areas. Mounted wildlife exhibits, and the real thing viewed through one-way windows, and a twenty-minute film are an excellent orientation. From there, climb the 90-foot observation tower, peer into the dark tannic waters from the boardwalk, and see some of the Okefenokee's three dozen varieties of reptiles at the Serpentarium.

Gate admission—$10.00 adults, $7.00 ages 6 to 11, free under 6—includes a 1½-mile guided boat tour and all exhibits and shows. A two-hour boat tour ($10.00 a person) includes an even more extensive look at the hundreds of species of birds, otter, armadillo, black bear, deer, and other critters who inhabit the swamp. You'll also see some of the 15,000 gators as they cruise among the reeds and cypresses like ironclad gunboats. (Back near the welcome center, you'll meet Oscar, the park's 15-foot, 900-pound mascot.)

If this two-hour sojourn was too brief, you may arrange with park officials for a guide who'll boat you back into really deep waters, where you may see what songwriter Stephen Foster only

Okefenokee Swamp Park

fantasized: the headwaters of the Suwannee River, which rise in the swamp and flow into Florida.

Okefenokee Swamp Park, Waycross 31501, (912) 283–0583, is open daily in spring and summer 9:00 A.M. to 6:30 P.M., fall and winter 9:00 A.M. to 5:30 P.M.

Two other attractions also mirror the swamp's colorful heritage. **Obediah's Okefenok** (912–287–0090), on a small island at the swamp's southwestern edge, was the early 1800s home of the Obediah Barber family. Their restored cabin and outbuildings are filled with authentic tools and household necessities. Open daily. Adults, $4.00; ages 4 to 17, $3.00.

The **Okefenokee Heritage Center,** (912) 285–4260, near downtown Waycross, is an indoor/outdoor museum with historical displays, art works, and a 1912 locomotive and depot, an 1840s farmhouse, a print shop, and antique vehicles. Open daily. Adults, $2.00; 18 and under, free. Phone (912) 285–4260.

Nearby ◆ **Laura S. Walker State Park,** Waycross 31501, (912) 287–4900, has campsites with water, electricity, showers, and rest rooms ($10.00 a night), a swimming pool, playground, fishing, and picnic tables. For reservations call (800) 864–PARK.

Waycross eateries invite you to enjoy fresh local fish and the exotic taste of alligator. **Ocean Galley Seafood's** "Swamp Platter" is heaped with fried 'gator tail, soft-shell crab, frog legs, turtle meat, and other Okefenokee fare. It's located at 421 memorial Drive, (912) 283–8341. **Adolph's Family Restaurant,** 410 Plant Avenue, (912) 283–1766, loads its buffet tables fried chicken, fish, fresh vegetables, salads, and other Southern favorites.

Contact Waycross/Ware County Chamber of Commerce, Box 137, Waycross 31502, (912) 287–4900, for more information.

Three gateways lead you into the primeval mysteries of the 412,000-acre **Okefenokee Swamp National Wildlife Refuge.** Suwannee Canal Recreation Area and Stephen C. Foster State Park are in Charlton County, while the Okefenokee Swamp Park is near Waycross, in Ware County.

Administered by the U.S. Fish and Wildlife Service, ◆ **Suwannee Canal Recreation Area** is what remains of one man's frustrated efforts to drain the Okefenokee back in the 1880s. He left behind an 11-mile-long waterway that now provides an easy avenue for boaters, fishermen, and sightseers. Along with boat

tours—one-hour trips are $7.50 for adults, $3.75 ages 5 to 11—
Suwannee Canal has several other visitor amenities.

The **Information Center Museum** has a fifteen-minute orientation film and exhibits of the swamp's plant and animal life.
A boardwalk over the water leads to a 50-foot observation platform. Picnic tables and rest rooms are clustered around the information center. The concession building stocks groceries, cold
drinks, insect repellents, and docks for guided boat tours.

. A short drive from the concession building and museum,
Chesser Island Homestead is the pine and cypress cabin once
home to several generations of the Chesser family.

Suwannee Canal Recreation Area, Route 2, Box 336, Folkston
31537, (912) 496–7156, is open daily sunrise to sunset. A $3.00
gate fee is charged at the Folkston entrance by the Okefenokee
National Wildlife Refuge. Drive on Highway 121/23 for 8 miles
south of Folkston, then turn right (west) at the Okefenokee
Refuge sign and continue 3 miles.

Overnight canoeing and two- to five-day wilderness canoeing
and camping adventures are available by advance reservations
from the Refuge Manager, Route 2, Box 338, Folkston 31537,
(912) 496–3331.

◆ **Stephen C. Foster State Park** is so far off Georgia's
beaten path that to get there from Suwannee Canal you'll have to
detour through northeastern Florida. From Suwannee Canal,
drive 15 miles south on Highway 23 to St. George, 37 miles west
on Highway 94 and Highway 2 in Florida, and back into Georgia
at Fargo. From Fargo, go right on Highway 177 and for 18 miles
cross a domain of sentinel pines and palmetto thickets, swampy
canals, egrets, great blue heron, deer, gators, armadillos, opos-
sum, raccoons, reptiles, and amphibians. Beyond a sign warning
that the gates close between sundown and sunup, you arrive at
Stephen Foster's compound.

The state park is an eighty-acre island entirely within the Okefenokee National Wildlife Refuge. Rangers conduct boat tours,
replete with swamp legends and lore, practical lessons in fauna
and flora, and lots of hilarious tall tales. You're bound to see
plenty of gators, exotic birds and plants, turtles, and trees. You
may also rent boats and canoes and venture forth on your own.
There are also a ¼-mile hiking trail, picnic shelters, a playground,
and small museum.

Staying overnight, serenaded by the symphony of the swamp,

is an unforgettable experience. Campsites with electricity, water, hot showers, and rest rooms are available as are two-bedroom cottages completely furnished with full kitchens and fireplaces, heat, and air-conditioning. There is a $2.00 per visit parking fee. The park's small grocery has minimal supplies, so be sure to stock up before leaving Fargo. You can calm your hunger for a long while with breakfast or lunch at **Arti C's Cafe,** on Highway 441, (912) 637–5227. The regular clientele are local loggers, so you'll get a whopping big plateful of hearty, rib-sticking chow for a very small price.

Stephen C. Foster State Park, Fargo 31631, (912) 637–5274, is open 7:00 A.M. to 7:00 P.M. from mid-September to the end of February and 6:30 A.M. to 8:30 P.M. from March 1 to mid-September. For cottage and camping reservations call (800) 864–PARK. When the gates are locked at night, only a dire emergency will open them before sunrise. This is done to protect you from roaming critters and the critters from roaming poachers. Also bear in mind that a swamp is full of mosquitoes, other biting pests, and uncomfortable summer heat and humidity. Bring insect repellent and dress comfortably.

In addition to the Folkston route, you may get to the park on Highway 441 to Fargo.

VALDOSTA AND THE GREAT SOUTHEAST

Depending on your perspective, **Lowndes County** is either the jumping-off place for Florida or your reentry point to Georgia. With 76,000 residents, Lowndes is Georgia's sixteenth most populous county. ◈ **Valdosta,** the county seat, with close to 50,000 residents, is the state's tenth largest city. With so much traffic flowing back and forth from Florida on I–75, much of the city is devoted to chain motels, fast-food strips, and factory outlet malls. Behind these contemporary distractions, under canopies of live oaks and palm trees and banks of azaleas and camellias, the city has many historic homes, churches, and public buildings.

Stop for free information and the **Historic Tours** self-guided map at the **Valdosta-Lowndes County Convention and Visitors Bureau's Tourism Information Center** off I–75 exit 5, 1703 Norman Drive, (912) 245–0513. Among the twenty-six landmarks, the most outstanding is ◈ **The Crescent.** Built in 1898, at a cost of $12,000 by Valdosta educator William S.

West, the grand twenty-three-room neo-classical mansion is graced by thirteen Doric columns supporting a crescent-shaped portico. In 1913 President Woodrow Wilson attended a gala dinner in the ballroom. Now maintained by the Valdosta Garden Center, the mansion has been restored to its original grandeur and appointed with many original furnishings and period antiques. The gardens are always in bloom. It's at 904 North Patterson Street, (912) 244-6747.

Before heading on, relax awhile at Valdosta's parks, boating and fishing lakes, and public golf courses and tennis courts.

The small Lowndes County town of **Hahira,** north of Valdosta at I-75 exit 7, is a center of Georgia's tobacco industry. From July to October you can witness the age-old ritual of tobacco auctioning at the town's warehouses. If you're here the first week of October, drop by the ❖ **Hahira Honeybee Festival.** To get the buzz on what's happening in town, and enjoy good home cooking, take a seat for breakfast or lunch at **The City Cafe** on Main Street. The Hahira Chamber of Commerce, Hahira 31632, (912) 794-2567, offers tobacco and honey tours.

At ❖ **Reed Bingham State Park,** off Highway 37, 6 miles west of Adel, the Cook County seat, you can go boating, fishing, waterskiing, and swimming on a 375-acre lake. The park also has a nature trail, campsites, and picnic grounds—and one rather unusual event. "Buzzard Day," the first Saturday of December, hails the thousands of buzzards that roost in the park each winter. Enjoy arts and crafts and musical entertainment while you watch the skies. Phone (912) 896-3551. For campsite reservations call (800) 864-PARK.

The ❖ **Jefferson Davis Memorial Museum,** Highway 32, in the small community of Irwinville, commemorates the site where the Confederate president was captured by Union troops on May 10, 1865. The museum has Civil War artifacts and part of the tree where Davis was standing when captured. A park around the museum has nature trails and picnic areas. Open Tuesday to Saturday 9:00 A.M. to 5:00 P.M., Sunday 1:00 to 5:00 P.M. Adults, $1.00; children, 50 cents. Phone (912) 831-2335.

After your history lesson, unwind at nearby ❖ **Crystal Lake Water Park,** which has a white sand beach, campsites, and boat rentals.

Tobacco, not java, is the economic lifeline of agrarian Coffee County. If you drop by the county seat of Douglas from midsummer through early fall, you'll see traffic jams of trucks bringing in leaf tobacco from across Southeast Georgia's "Tobacco Belt." The gold leaf is auctioned in the age-old tradition at warehouses around the town and sent off for cigarettes, pipe and chewing tobacco, and snuff. After the hullabaloo of the auction houses, unwind a while at two tranquil recreation areas.

◆ **General Coffee State Park,** on Highway 32, 6 miles east of Douglas, offers a wealth of recreational opportunities. You can fish the lake and streams for catfish, gar, and bream and swim in the outdoor pool. A nature trail winding through the wooded 1,490-acre park puts you in photo range of many species of birds, reptiles, deer, and other critters. There are also playgrounds and picnic shelters. You can stay overnight in full-service campsites and in a group cabin sleeping thirty-six. Phone (912) 384–7082. For camping and cabin reservations call (800) 864–PARK.

In Douglas, which is a pretty college town of 15,000 folks, you can either play the 18-hole ◆ **Beaver Kreek Golf Club** course, (912) 384–8230, or you might want to try your swing at the 9-hole ◆ **Community Golf Course,** (912) 384–7353. Rental clubs are available at both. After your round, drive into Douglas's revived downtown area—it's one of Georgia's Main Street Program cities—and enjoy lunch or dinner at **Fern Bank Bar and Grill,** (912) 422–7828, an historic brick-walled building with good steaks, seafood, and Southern dishes and many relics from the city's past.

The small town of **Fitzgerald** (pop. 8,600) is a living memorial to the nation's post–Civil War reunification. In the 1890s Indiana newspaper publisher P. H. Fitzgerald envisioned a place where he and other Union veterans could live in peace with their former Southern foes. When Ben Hill County farmers sent trainloads of food in response to a Midwestern drought, it became the chosen place. The town was laid out on a grid, with streets on the west side named for Confederate generals, those on the east side for Union generals. Other streets were named for Northern and Southern trees and flowers.

The ◆ **Blue and Gray Museum,** in the former train depot, displays thousands of Civil War artifacts, including uniforms, weapons, newspaper articles about Lincoln's assassination, and a history of this unique town. It's open April 1 to October 1, Monday to Friday 2:00 to 5:00 P.M. Free admission. Phone (912) 423-5375.

Until July 4, 1986, most motorists passed through the little Telfair County seat of McRae without a second thought. Nowadays, they have a reason to stop, get out of their cars, and take a picture. Right in the middle of town, where Highways 341, 441, 280, 23, and 319 come together, there's a replica of the ◆ **Statue of Liberty,** a **Liberty Bell,** and copies of the **Declaration of Independence,** the **Constitution,** and other documents. "Miss Liberty" stands 32 feet tall—a $\frac{1}{12}$th-scale reproduction of the original in New York Harbor. And she's entirely homemade. Her head is carved from a black gum tree, her torch from cypress, her fiberglass coating created by a McRae boat manufacturer.

McRae's most popular eateries are **The Depot Restaurant** in the center of town, (912) 868–5930, specializing in Southern home cooking plate lunches and dinners and an ample Friday night seafood buffet; and **Knowles B-B-Que** off Highway 341, south of town, (912) 868–2946. ◆ **Little Ocmulgee State Park and Pete Phillips Lodge and Convention Center,** off Highway 441, 2 miles north of McRae, is a resort park with lots of things to keep you happily occupied. You can challenge the park's well-maintained 18-hole, par-72 golf course and rent carts and clubs at the pro shop. You can also swim, play tennis, and hike nature trails. Pete Phillips Lodge and Conference Center has thirty modern motel-type guest rooms, an outdoor pool, a full-service restaurant, and meeting rooms. You can also pitch your tent or park your RV in full service campsites and stay in furnished cottages. For camping, cottage, and lodge reservations phone (800) 864–PARK. For general information contact the Park Superintendent, P.O. Box 149, McRae 31055, (912) 868–7474.

NORTHWEST GEORGIA

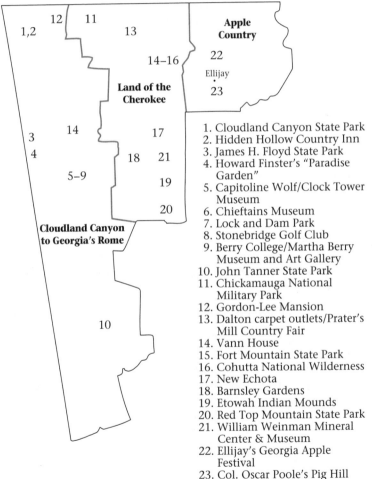

12 11
1,2 13

Apple Country

22

14–16

Ellijay
•
23

Land of the Cherokee

14
3
4
18 21

5–9

19

20

Cloudland Canyon to Georgia's Rome

10

1. Cloudland Canyon State Park
2. Hidden Hollow Country Inn
3. James H. Floyd State Park
4. Howard Finster's "Paradise Garden"
5. Capitoline Wolf/Clock Tower Museum
6. Chieftains Museum
7. Lock and Dam Park
8. Stonebridge Golf Club
9. Berry College/Martha Berry Museum and Art Gallery
10. John Tanner State Park
11. Chickamauga National Military Park
12. Gordon-Lee Mansion
13. Dalton carpet outlets/Prater's Mill Country Fair
14. Vann House
15. Fort Mountain State Park
16. Cohutta National Wilderness
17. New Echota
18. Barnsley Gardens
19. Etowah Indian Mounds
20. Red Top Mountain State Park
21. William Weinman Mineral Center & Museum
22. Ellijay's Georgia Apple Festival
23. Col. Oscar Poole's Pig Hill of Fame

NORTHWEST GEORGIA

CLOUDLAND CANYON TO GEORGIA'S ROME

◆ **Cloudland Canyon State Park,** in far northwest Georgia's remote and rugged Dade County, contains one of the Southeast's most awesome natural sights. The park's namesake and centerpiece is a steep canyon cut into the western flank of Lookout Mountain by **Sitton Creek Gulch.** You may stand by the rim and peer into misty reaches 1,800 feet deep. Better still, lace up your hiking boots, follow woodland trails down to three waterfalls on the canyon floor, and get really off the beaten path on 6 miles of backcountry trails.

After you hike, unwind with a swim in the park pool or a few quick sets of tennis. Also in the heavily forested 2,120-acre park are sixteen completely furnished cottages and seventy-five tent and trailer sites, with electrical and water connections, showers, and rest rooms. For camping and cottage reservations call (800) 864–PARK. Contact Park Superintendent, Route 2, Box 150, Rising Fawn 30738, (706) 657–4050.

According to tradition, Cherokee Indians named their children for symbolic signs that caught their eye after birth. So the Cloudland community of **Rising Fawn** owes its poetic name to a chief who legend says looked out of his lodge on the happy morning his son was born and saw a newborn fawn wobble to its feet by its mother's side.

After a vigorous day in the park, make tracks for **Geneva Wooten's Restaurant,** (706) 398–1749. Across Highway 136 from the Cloudland entrance, the homey cafe is the eating-meeting-greeting destination for folks from miles around. At breakfast, lunch, and dinner, country cooking just doesn't get any better.

◆ **Hidden Hollow Country Inn,** 5 miles down the mountain from Cloudland Canyon, is one of those discoveries you can hardly wait to tell your best friends about. Tommy and Bonnie Jean Thomas preside over a gaggle of rustic but very comfortable family-size cabins around a small lake full of Canada geese. Cabins are filled with well-worn furniture, cards, board games, dog-eared magazines, coffee, but there are no TVs or phones to ruffle your peaceful ruminations. For entertainment snag a fish in the lake, hike in the woods, and watch the sun come up and go down.

Two persons are $55–$75, $8 for each additional. No meals are served, but Geneva Wooten's and other restaurants are close by. The inn is at 463 Hidden Hollow Lane, Chickamauga 30707, (706) 539–2372.

Be sure to bring your fishing gear when you head for ◆ **James H. Floyd State Park.** Off Highway 27, 3 miles southeast of the Chattooga County seat of Summerville, the 270-acre park is renowned as one of the state's finest fishing places. A pair of stocked lakes—thirty and thirty-five acres—offer excellent bass-fishing opportunities from the banks. Only boats with trolling motors are allowed.

Area fishermen say you can expect to reel in impressive large-mouth bass, as well as big catches of catfish and bream. Young-sters can learn some of the fine arts of fishing during the park's annual fishing rodeo in mid-May. Admission is free, and prizes are awarded for the first, largest, and most fish caught.

Floyd State Park's twenty-five tent and trailer sites have water and electrical hookups and convenient showers and rest rooms. You'll also find a playground, picnic areas, and hiking trails in the neighboring Chattahoochee National Forest. Contact Park Superintendent, Route 1, Summerville 30747, (706) 857–0826. Call (800) 864–PARK for camping reservations.

Three miles north of Summerville, turn right off U.S. Highway 27 onto Rena Street (between Jim's Auto Supply and Penn Auto Parts) and prepare for an otherworldly visit to ◆ **Howard Finster's "Paradise Garden,"** (706) 857–2926. One of America's premier folk artists, Reverend Finster made his garden a jumble of gaudily painted angels, birds, animals, 14-foot Coke bottles, heaven-bound buses, surreal images of Elvis and Marilyn Monroe—and everywhere you look, biblical passages and admonitions. Paintings and wooden figures by Finster, his son, and grandson sell from $20 to $2,500. The garden is open daily 9:00 A.M. to 5:00 P.M.

Like its Italian counterpart, Georgia's Rome spreads over seven green hills, in the foothills of the state's northwestern Appalachian Mountains. In the rivers department, the Georgia city of 30,000 has the edge. Instead of one mere Tiber, the Floyd County seat has three: the Etowah and Oostanaula, which join up downtown and form the Coosa. It may not have personages to match the Caesars, but a *dramatis personae* of Cherokee Indian chieftains, Southern aristocrats, cotton traders, Civil War soldiers, and riverboat paddle wheelers have made a rich and colorful cast, all the same. The city got its name quite by chance. In 1834 two traveling salesmen and a cotton planter put their choice of names in a hat. "Rome" was the fortuitous choice, otherwise the city might be known today as Warsaw or Hamburg. A revitalized downtown, focusing on the three rivers, ensures Rome of a future as exciting as its past.

Begin your Roman holiday at the Greater Rome Visitors Center (706) 295–5576 or (800) 444–1834, a rejuvenated Southern Railway passenger depot, circa 1900, and a retired caboose at 402 Civic Center Drive, off Highway 20 and Highway 27 near downtown. Information is available Monday through Friday 9:00 A.M. to 5:00 P.M., Saturday 10:00 A.M. to 3:00 P.M., Sunday noon to 3:00 P.M.

"The Between the Rivers Walking Tour"—it can also be driven, of course—leads you past thirty-eight historic downtown landmarks. If you've been to the Italian Rome, you'll probably recognize the statue in front of City Hall here. The ◆ **Capitoline Wolf,** a replica of the Etruscan sculpture on ancient Rome's Capitoline Hill, depicts the city's mythical founders, Romulus and Remus, being nurtured by a she-wolf. It was a 1929 goodwill gift from Benito Mussolini.

The **Town Clock,** on Clock Tower Hill, is the city's symbol and one of its most beloved landmarks. Built in Waltham, Massachusetts, in 1871, the four 9-foot-diameter clock faces top a handsome brick and cypress water tower. So many people wanted to climb the 104-foot tower that the city opened it as the ◆ **Clock Tower Museum.** You can walk up the spiral staircase and take in panoramic views of the city's hills and rivers. Also admire the handsomely restored clock works and murals depicting chapters in the city's history. It's open Saturday 10:00 A.M. to 4:00 P.M. and Sunday 1:00 to 5:00 P.M. from April to November and other times by appointment. Free admission. Phone (706) 236–4416.

Myrtle Hill Cemetery, on another of the city's seven hills, is a beautiful tree-shaded sanctuary where Mrs. Woodrow Wilson, 377 Confederate soldiers, and other notables are buried. You're welcome to stroll and admire the panoramic views of Rome's rivers and green hills.

Until recently the Etowah, Oostanaula, and Coosa had to flood before Romans would pay them any attention. Nowadays the 2.5-mile **Heritage Trail** walking, biking, and hiking route, shaded by big trees, takes inhabitants and visitors along the Oostanaula from the **Rome–Floyd County Public Library** downtown to the ◆ **Chieftains Museum.** If you'd like to get out on the water, the visitors bureau can direct you to a canoe rental.

You can also unwind at ◆ **Lock and Dam Park,** a publicly owned camping/RV/fishing/boating park in a mountain setting beside a 1910 lock on the Coosa River. Facilities include twenty-five fully equipped RV campsites, fishing pier, canoe rentals, boat ramp and docks, bait shop, and snack bar. Call (404) 234–5001 for information.

If golf's your game, check out the new ◆ **Stonebridge Golf Club,** (706) 236–4400. Owned by the city of Rome, the 18-hole par-72, 6,971-yard layout is at the base of Lavendar Mountain, on the Berry College grounds. Rolling fairways, water, and big stands of hardwoods and pines are scenic to look at and challenging to play. The course is named for an old stone bridge over a lake on the ninth fairway. Greens fees won't handicap your budget: $18 weekdays, $24 weekends, plus $10 cart fee.

Two historic homes invite bed-and-breakfast guests. **Chandler Arms Bed & Breakfast,** 2 Coral Avenue, Rome 30161, (706) 235–5702 or (800) 438–9492, is infused with the English hospitality and effervescent personality of innkeeper Rosemary Chandler, a transplanted Brit. Each guest room in her 1902 Victorian home has a different turn-of-the-century motif and private bath. The Honeymoon Suite has a brass canopy bed and whirlpool. Full English breakfast, afternoon high tea, and wind-down wine enhance the gracious ambience. Doubles are $60–$75.

Claremont House Bed & Breakfast, 906 East Second Avenue, Rome 30161, (706) 291–0900 and (800) 254–4797, is a showplace Victorian Gothic mansion built in 1882. Innkeeper Patsy Priest has lavished her public spaces and guest rooms with antiques, wood-burning fireplaces, and elaborately carved woodwork. Champagne in the parlor, rocking chairs on the verandas, and full gourmet breakfast served in the dining room are part of the experience of this historic downtown home. Doubles are $60–$80.

The Chieftains Museum is Rome's oldest historical landmark. Built as a frontier log cabin in 1794, Chieftains was the home of Major Ridge, the Cherokee leader who signed a treaty with the U.S. government that partially contributed to the explusion of the Cherokees from Georgia and the tragic "Trail of Tears." Along with Cherokee history, the museum's artifacts tell the story of

Rome as a river town and its role in the antebellum South and the Civil War. An open archaeological dig and a nineteenth-century riverboat are on the grounds. It's at 80 Chatillon Road, off Highway 27, (706) 291–9494. Hours are Tuesday through Friday 11:00 A.M. to 4:00 P.M.; Sunday 2:00 to 5:00 P.M.

Rome's most inspiring personality was a determined lady named Martha Berry. Born to privilege in a white-columned Greek Revival mansion, Miss Berry in 1902 founded the Berry Schools to provide educational opportunities to impoverished Appalachian youth. Her original domain of 83 acres has grown to 28,000 acres of handsome buildings, forests, fields, mountains, lakes, and streams. Many students of today's ❖ **Berry College** earn their tuition by working on the college's farm, research facilities, and other enterprises.

"The Miracle of the Mountains" is chronicled at the ❖ **Martha Berry Museum and Art Gallery,** across from the campus on Highway 27. You'll see a twenty-eight-minute film on her remarkable life and achievements and photos, furniture, and memorabilia. Nearby **Oak Hill** (706–232–5374), built in 1847, is the classic Old South mansion, filled with the Berry family's antiques and artworks. Behind the museum, an easygoing nature trail loops through woodlands, ponds, and native plants. Around Oak Hill, you're free to wander five acres of tiered formal gardens. The Martha Berry Museum and Oak Hill are open Tuesday through Saturday 10:00 A.M. to 5:00 P.M. and Sunday 1:00 to 5:00 P.M. Admission is adults $3.00, students $1.50, under age 6 free.

You're welcome to drive through what's proudly called, "The World's Most Beautiful Campus." Among the Berry College landmarks are the **Ford Buildings,** a cluster of handsome English Gothic structures and a reflecting pool donated by Henry Ford. In the Ford Buildings' **Weaving Room,** students perpetuate a mountain craft revived by Miss Berry. During the week you can watch as afghans, rugs, placemats, and jackets are hand-loomed the ages-old way. These beautiful pieces, and student-made pottery and glassware, sell for $5 to $125. If you keep seeing a familiar face you just can't place, it's probably Berry's Museum director, Dan Biggers, who plays the coroner on TV's *In the Heat of the Night* and appears in other series filmed in Georgia.

You're also invited to visit the scenic campuses of **Shorter**

Berry College

College and **Darlington Lower School,** neighbors on Shorter Avenue west of downtown.

If you'd like to get a little lost in the woods, make an appointment to visit **Marshall Forest,** on Horseleg Creek Road, off Highway 20, 4 miles west of downtown. The lush 170-acre preserve, administered by the Georgia Conservancy, includes ninety acres of fields and eighty acres of forests, where northern red and chestnut oaks mingle with long leaf southern pines. About 300 species of wildflowers and other plants grow on the Flower Glen Trail. The Big Pine Braille Trail offers blind visitors the opportunity to stop at twenty stations describing fifty-three plant species, thirty-one species of trees, and nineteen species of vines and shrubs. Call the Rome Visitor Center for information, (800) 444–1834.

Cave Spring, a village of 950 residents and one traffic light 16 miles south of Rome (via Highway 411), is pure Norman Rockwell. The **Hearn House B & B,** a comfy community-owned inn in an 1840s schoolhouse, features five guest rooms with private bath and breakfast for $50–$60 per night. When you're well rested, lace up your walking shoes and head across **Rolater Park** to the limestone cave that gave the town its name. Inside the caverns you'll see the spring whose pure water is bottled and sold in area stores.

Around the square more than a dozen antiques stores and flea markets are a collector's dream. Some of the nicest include **Asbury House** (706–777–3608); **Martha Jane's Fudge, Gifts and Collectibles** (706–777–3608); and **Christa's Etc.** (706–777–3586). More than a hundred artists and craftspeople come for the **Cave Spring Arts Festival** the second weekend of June. For information and bed-and-breakfast reservations, contact City of Cave Spring, P.O. Box 365, Cave Spring 30124, (706) 777–3382.

❖ **John Tanner State Park,** off Highway 16, 6 miles west of Carrollton, is a popular getaway for west Georgians and east Alabamians. Six furnished one-bedroom cottages and thirty-six full-service campsites surround a lake with a sandy swimming beach, rental fishing boats, and tree-shaded picnic shelters. Contact Park Superintendent, 354 Tanners Beach Road, Carrollton 30117, (770) 830–2222. For campsite and cottage reservations, call (800) 864–PARK.

LAND OF THE CHEROKEE

In the hellish heat of September 19 and 20, 1863, nearly 130,000 Americans engaged in one of the bloodiest battles of the entire Civil War. When it was over, Confederate forces under the command of General Braxton Bragg had a costly and dubious victory. They had repulsed the outnumbered Union armies under General William Rosecrans but were too weakened to pursue the Federals as they fled to safety around Chattanooga, Tennessee. Subsequent Union victories at Chattanooga's Lookout Mountain and Missionary Ridge and the capture of the city's vital railway hub opened General William T. Sherman's route to Atlanta and the sea.

The 5,500-acre Chickamauga battlefield is now part of the Chattanooga and ◆ **Chickamauga National Military Park.** The major sites are adjacent to Highway 27, near Chattanooga and Chickamauga. Stop first at the National Park Service Visitors Center for the audiovisual orientation and the many exhibits. The **Fuller Collection of Military Arms** has more than 400 weapons from the French and Indian Wars through present-day conflicts.

Park rangers in Civil War uniforms demonstrate cannon and rifles. The Chattanooga Symphony Orchestra has free outdoor concerts on summer Sunday evenings. Bring a blanket and a picnic supper and join the festivities!

From the visitors center, follow Highway 27 for 3 miles through the park. Battle sites are marked by earthworks, cannon batteries, and farm buildings. Impressive monuments have been placed by states whose sons in blue and gray died here more than 125 years ago. The park is open all the time. The visitors center is open daily from 8:00 A.M. to 5:45 P.M. Contact Park Superintendent, P.O. Box 2128, Ft. Oglethorpe 30742, (706) 866-9241.

The ◆ **Gordon-Lee Mansion,** on the edge of the battlefield park, invites you to spend the night in antebellum luxury. Built in 1847, the white-columned Greek Revival residence served as Union headquarters and a hospital during the battle. Guest rooms and public areas are furnished with Civil War–era antiques. Rates of $70–$95 per night include evening wine and cheese on the veranda and a continental-plus breakfast. Contact Gordon-Lee Mansion, 217 Cove Road, Chickamauga 30707, (706) 375-4728.

Before leaving the area, see **Lookout Mountain, Missionary Ridge,** and other major parts of the Chattanooga and Chickamauga National Military Park.

If you've been planning to recarpet your home or cover your pool deck or patio with Astroturf, put off that major purchase until you've been to **Dalton.** Seat of northwest Georgia's green and hilly Whitfield County, industrious Dalton, with a population of 25,000, is the long-reigning "Carpet Capital of the World."

About 66 percent of all the tufted carpeting manufactured in the United States rolls off the giant looms of Dalton's more than seventy-five modern plants. If you're in a buying frame of mind or would just enjoy browsing the latest styles and colors, dozens of ❖ **Dalton carpet outlets** offer a full range of floor coverings at greatly reduced prices. The Dalton Convention and Visitors Bureau, off I-75 exit 136 at 524 Holiday Drive, (706) 278-7373, can provide you with an up-to-date outlets directory. You can also find out about guided tours of area mills.

Dalton's $5-billion carpeting industry was born around 1900, when a Whitfield County farm girl named Catherine Evans produced a hand-tufted chenille bedspread, copied from a family heirloom, and promptly sold it for the handsome price of $2.50. Encouraged by her success, she made more of the brightly colored cotton bedspreads, and these, too, were eagerly snapped up by tourists and local homemakers. Other homebound women began following her lead, and by the early 1920s, tufted bedspreads had grown into a major "cottage industry."

The bedspreads usually featured flowers and other patterns, but the brilliantly plumed male peacock was such a runaway favorite that Highway 41, the major highway leading into Dalton, became popularly known as "Peacock Alley."

In the 1920s, a machine invented in Dalton was able to mass-produce the cotton bedspreads. Another wizard soon realized that by tufting more densely and adding a sturdy backing the same machinery could be adapted to the manufacture of carpeting. Dalton—and households the world over—were never again the same.

The original "cottage craft" of chenille bedspreads is still alive. You can find a practical souvenir with a peacock, Elvis Presley, Jesus Christ, the Confederate battle flag, and other designs at stores around Dalton and along Highway 41—the original "Peacock Alley"—between Dalton and the Tennessee border. Figure on paying a bit more than $2.50, however!

Some of the early chenille bedspreads are among the exhibits at **Crown Gardens and Archives,** in the original Crown Cotton Mill at 715 Chattanooga Avenue, (706) 278–0217. The museum also has historical displays, a Black heritage room, an outdoor spring, and picnic areas. It's open Tuesday to Sunday. Admission is free.

With its influx of executives and workers from across the nation and several foreign countries, this surprisingly cosmopolitan little city is very active in the fine arts. The **Creative Arts Guild,** 520 West Waugh Street, (706) 278–0168, is a tastefully contemporary complex with two art galleries and a forum for live theater, dance, and other cultural programs. It's open daily. Admission is free.

Dalton is also a festive city. The **Red Carpet Festival,** the first weekend of May, celebrates Dalton's famous industry with parades, pageantry, square dancing, bluegrass and gospel music, and plenty of barbecue and other hearty Southern cooking.

On the second weekend of May and October, the ◆ **Prater's Mill Country Fair** centers on Benjamin Franklin Prater's circa 1859 grist mill. While the huge millstones turn out silky cornmeal, 185 artists and craftsmen sell their wares to the tune of bluegrass fiddlers, clog dancers, and gospel singers. There are pony rides and other special treats just for the youngsters.

To get the scoop on what's happening in town, drop by **The Oakwood Cafe,** downtown at 201 West Cuyler Street, (706) 278–4421. Legions of Daltonians wouldn't think about starting their day without Oakwood omelets, hot cakes, and ham and sausage biscuits. They're back at lunch and dinner for steaks, chicken, chops, and seafood. Breakfast, lunch, and dinner are served Monday to Saturday.

Dalton Depot Restaurant & Trackside Cafe, 110 Depot Street, five minutes from I-75, (706) 226–3160, is the carpet city's liveliest eating and drinking address. The cleverly regeared old wooden train depot has a something-for-everyone menu: Stuffed jalapeños and quesadillas, filet mignon, baby back ribs, prime rib, ribeye and sirloin steak, chicken several different ways, fish and shrimp, sandwiches and salads, and bar drinks and 130 brands of beer. Lunch and dinner are served Monday to Saturday.

When Daltonites are in the mood for a dress-up dinner, they head for **The Cellar Restaurant and Lounge** in the Dalton

Shopping Center, 1331 West Walnut Avenue, (706) 226–6029. Veal, seafood, steaks, soups, salads, cocktails, and wines are served at lunch, Monday through Friday, and dinner, Monday through Saturday, at moderate prices.

◆ **Vann House** was a showplace of nineteenth-century Cherokee accomplishment. At the junction of Highways 52 and 225, 3 miles west of modern-day Chatsworth, the sturdy three-story house, with brick walls 2-feet thick, was built in modified Georgian style in 1804–1805. Owner James Vann was a half-Cherokee, half-Scot who helped create a Moravian mission for the education of young Cherokees. When Vann died in 1809, his son Joseph inherited the house and surrounding farmlands. He prospered until 1830, when the state of Georgia confiscated his lands for violating a law forbidding white men to work for Indians.

The Georgia Department of Natural Resources has restored the house and refurnished and redecorated the rooms in early-nineteenth-century style. An intricately carved "floating staircase" is one of Georgia's earliest surviving examples of cantilevered construction. Elsewhere are Bibles, dinnerware, and dining room and bedroom furnishings. Vann House, Chatsworth 30705, (706) 695–2598, is open Tuesday through Saturday 9:00 A.M. to 5:00 P.M., Sunday 2:00 to 5:30 P.M. Adults are $2.00; ages 6 to 18, $1.00; under 6, free.

On Highway 52, 7 miles east of Chatsworth, ◆ **Fort Mountain State Park** is a superscenic park on a forested, 2,800-foot peak of the Blue Ridge Mountains' Cohutta Range. The park's namesake is a puzzling rock wall, or foundation, that winds nearly 900 feet around the mountainside. Whether it was an ancient Indian fortress, a bastion built by twelfth-century Welsh explorers, or part of some other inscrutable mission is a matter of speculation. The stone observation tower nearby is no mystery. It's a legacy of the Depression-era Civilian Conservation Corps (CCC).

History lessons aside, you may relax in Fort Mountain's lake, hike nature trails, play miniature golf, and set the kids loose on the playground. The 115 campsites have water, electricity, hot showers, and rest rooms. Fifteen two- and three-bedroom cottages come with kitchen appliances, towels, sheets, and logs for the fireplace. Contact Park Superintendent, Chatsworth 30705, (706) 695–2621. For reservations call (800) 864–PARK.

You can really get off the beaten path by plunging into the nearby ◆ **Cohutta National Wilderness,** 34,000 acres of mountains, forests, and rivers. Contact the U.S. Forest Service, 401 Old Ellijay Road, Chatsworth 30705, (706) 695–6736.

The best home cooking in these parts is at **Edna's Cafe** on Highway 441 in Chatsworth, (706) 695–4951, which puts out a superb lunch Monday through Saturday. Don't miss the coconut and peanut butter pie!

The Cherokee Indians assimilated themselves into the way of life established by the white settlers, then were ruthlessly crushed at ◆ **New Echota,** near modern-day Calhoun. In the 1820s New Echota was laid out as the capital of the Cherokee Nation that included parts of Georgia, the Carolinas, Tennessee, and Alabama. Here, the Cherokee legislature formulated laws, enforced by a series of district courts and a supreme court. The Indians wore European-style dress, used the farming methods of the white settlers, and lived in stone and frame houses with the most modern conveniences of the day. The more affluent owned black slaves. The first North American tribe to formulate their own written alphabet, the Cherokee published a bilingual newspaper, circulated as far as Europe.

Gold discovered on Cherokee lands in the late 1820s brought it all to disaster. Supported by President Andrew Jackson, the state of Georgia confiscated all Cherokee lands and in 1838 forced the Indians into exile in what is now Oklahoma. Thousands perished along this "Trail of Tears."

New Echota has been meticulously reconstructed as a state historic site. Stop first to see the orientation slide show and exhibits in the reception center. Then take a self-guided walking tour that includes the Supreme Court Building, the printing presses of the *Cherokee Phoenix* newspaper, a tavern/general store, and the home of the Reverend Samuel Worcester, a Massachusetts minister who established a mission for the Indians. Park rangers frequently demonstrate arrowhead making and hunting techniques. Books about the Cherokee civilization are on sale at the reception center. In late October the **Cherokee Fall Festival** is a weekend of Indian crafts, cooking, and storytelling.

New Echota, Route 3, Calhoun 30701, (706) 629–8151, is open Tuesday through Saturday 9:00 A.M. to 5:00 P.M., and Sunday 2:00 to 5:30 P.M. Adults are $2.00; ages 6 to 18, 75 cents; under 6, free.

New Echota

After all this history, replenish your energy at **B.J.'s Restaurant,** in a small shopping center at 102 Bryant Parkway (Highway 41), south of downtown Calhoun, (706) 629–3461. Luncheon specialties include chicken pot pie, barbecue, country fried steak, and vegetables; dinner features seafood, steaks, and pasta.

You may combine New Echota's fascinating lessons with Vann House in neighboring Murray County and the Etowah Indian Mounds, near Cartersville in Bartow County.

Bartow County, along I–75 between Atlanta and Chattanooga, is the site of a fascinating Indian temple mound complex. Here, also, you can visit a small gem of a mineral museum and take a minivacation at a state park on a 12,000-acre lake.

❖ **Barnsley Gardens,** 10 miles west of I–75 Adairsville exit 128, (770) 773–7480, was created in the 1840s by Englishman Godfrey Barnsley and features thousands of acres of gardens, cultivated trees, and orchards centered on a twenty-eight-room Italianate manor house. Following Barnsley's death in 1873, the estate fell into ruins and weeds. Then, in 1990, a Bavarian aristocrat purchased the remaining 1,300 acres and brought Barnsley Gardens back to life. Visitors now can stroll through a wildflower meadow, a hillside with hundreds of flowering rhododendrons, and along a colorful perennial border. The boxwood parterre in front of the manor house ruins is graced by an ornamental fountain with a likeness of Barnsley's wife Julia, who, some say, still wanders in the gardens. The Gardens Restaurant, open daily except Monday, serves lunch Tuesday to Sunday and dinner Friday and Saturday. Admission is $6.50 for adults; senior citizens, $5.75; students, $4.00; and ages 12 and under, free.

Between A.D. 1000 and 1500, the Etowah Indian tribe migrated into the fertile Etowah River Valley, near today's Cartersville, and created a remarkably sophisticated culture. Beans, squash, corn, and fruit that the women cultivated complemented game trapped by the men in surrounding forests and the abundant fish in the Etoway. As part of a fast trading network, the Etowahs made tools, arrowheads, axes, and household implements from Great Lakes copper and Mississippi and Ohio Valley flint. Gulf Coast seashells were fashioned into ceremonial jewelry.

Surrounded by a deep moat and log stockade, a compact city of clay and wooden houses sheltered as many as 4,000 Indians. The heart of the city was half a dozen rectangular earthen mounds.

77

The ❖ **Etowah Indian Mounds** were the forum for religious rites conducted by chiefs and priests and the final resting place of these dignitaries.

Stop first at the excellent small museum and reception center, where dioramas and artifacts from the mounds tell the story of this mysteriously vanished tribe. The exhibits are highlighted by a priest's burial chamber and beautifully carved busts of a woman and a warrior. A film traces the history of the Etowahs. With a diagrammed map, cross the moat and explore the grass-covered mounds. Ninety-two steps take you up 63 feet to the top of Mound "A," from which the priest conducted rituals for the townspeople assembled below in the plaza. Mound "C," one of the smallest, was a principal burial site and the source of most of the artifacts in the museum. Park rangers periodically lead moonlight walks around the site.

About a fifteen-minute drive west of I–75 exit 124, via Highway 113/61, Etowah Mounds State Historic Site, Route 1, Cartersville 30120, (706) 387–3747, is open Tuesday through Saturday 9:00 A.M. to 5:00 P.M. and Sunday 2:00 to 5:30 P.M. Adults are $2.00; ages 6 to 8, 75 cents; under 6, free.

In Cartersville, a congenial town of 10,000, you may want to walk around the downtown shopping area and admire the stately **Bartow County Courthouse. Etowah Arts Gallery,** 13 Wall Street, (706) 382–8277, sells pottery, paintings, handmade quilts, and other crafts by local artists. **Morrell's,** a homey, family-run restaurant a quarter-mile off I–75 exit 125, (770) 382–1222, is a popular destination for fried chicken, steaks, children's plates, and Southern breakfast daily.

❖ **Red Top Mountain State Park,** on exit 123 off I–75 south of Cartersville, is one of the nicest and prettiest in the whole system. A wealth of recreational opportunities, campsites, and cottages are spread over the wooded hillsides around 12,000-acre Lake Allatoona. During warm weather, you may sun on a sandy beach, swim, and waterski. The rest of the year, bring tennis racquets, fishing gear, picnic supplies, and hiking shoes. Boaters may bring their own or rent houseboats and pontoon boats at the park marina. A small grocery is at the reception center.

Red Top's twenty two-bedroom cottages are completely furnished and include fireplaces. The 286 camping sites have electricity, water, hot showers, and rest rooms. The park's new Red Top Mountain Lodge has thirty-three modern guest rooms in a quiet cove with a full-service restaurant. The park office is open daily from 8:00 A.M. to 5:00 P.M. Contact Superintendent, Cartersville 30120, (770) 975–0055. Call (800) 864–PARK for camping, cottage, and lodge reservations.

North of Cartersville, less than a mile from I–75 exit 126, the attractive, well-planned ❖ **William Weinman Mineral Center & Museum** is an intriguing stopover for rockhounds and other nature-lovers. Gemstones, minerals, fossils, crystals, arrowheads, geodes, and other specimens are displyed in brightly lighted glass cases. Some are from right here in northwest Georgia's own mineral-mining regions; others are imports from South America, Africa, Australia, Mexico, and the Western United States.

In a simulated limestone cave, with authentic stalactites and stalagmites, you can trace the eons-long formation of caves with easy-to-follow diagrams and explanations. The cave's treasures also include a mastodon's sixty-pound molar and a fossilized box turtle. Other exhibits include a huge array of Indian arrowheads and flint weapons, fluorescent minerals, petrified wood, brilliantly polished geodes, rock crystal, and colorful birthstones. Books, jewelry, and mineral samples are for sale in the gift shop.

The museum, Cartersville 30120, (770) 386–0576, is open Tuesday through Saturday 10:00 A.M. to 4:30 P.M. and Sunday 2:00 to 4:30 P.M. Adults, $3.00; ages 6 to 12, $2.00; 5 and under, no charge.

APPLE COUNTRY

Gilmer County, in the Blue Ridge Mountains about ninety minutes due north of metro Atlanta, is "Georgia's Apple Capital." Dozens of orchards dotting the county's green mountainsides annually produce more than 300,000 bushels of Granny Smiths, Red and Golden Delicious, Yates, Jonathans, Stayman Winesaps, Rome Beauties, and exotic Asian newcomers such as Fujis and Mutsus. In the fall, when the trees are loaded with fruit, visitors by the thousands are invited into the orchards to pick their own basketsful. Those who'd just as soon leave the labor to somebody else can buy all they can haul home at farm stores that line the highways leading to **Ellijay,** the Gilmer County seat. They also can take away freshly squeezed apple cider, apple pies and cakes, and recipe books to prepare just about everything with apples.

79

To celebrate the harvest, ◆ **Ellijay's Georgia Apple Festival,** two weekends in mid-October, puts on parades, apple pie-eating and apple-cooking contests, arts and crafts, mountain music and dancing, and a host of other festivities. Ellijay is a delightful small town with 1,700 amiable inhabitants. It may remind you of Sheriff Andy Taylor's bucolic hometown of Mayberry. To find out what's going on—and enjoy some delicious home cooking—stop by the **Calico Cupboard** on the courthouse square, (706) 635–7575, and tuck into grits, biscuits, and sausage at breakfast time, and fried chicken, fried fish, biscuits, and vegetables at lunchtime, with a whopping big slice of apple cobbler, of course. Walk it off with a stroll around the corner to **Penland Brothers Store,** a bona fide general merchandise emporium, which has been supplying Gilmer Countians with all their necessities since 1913. Several antiques and craft shops are also around the square.

When your appetite's worked up again, get ready for some serious barbecue. As you drive into town on the four-lane Zell Miller Mountain Parkway (Highway 515), you can't help but notice ◆ **Col. Oscar Poole's Pig Hill of Fame.** For $5.00, you, too, can have your name painted on one of thousands of little plywood piggies that graze on the hillside beside Col. Poole's yolk-yellow **Real Pit Bar-B-Q** establishment, (706) 635–4100. (Col. Poole is also a Methodist minister, and your $5.00 goes to church missions.) Inside, the barbecue is seriously delicious.

In contrast to Col. Poole's flamboyant stand, you'll have to look closely to find **Holloway's Pink Pig,** (706) 276–1700, on Highway 515 in the community of Cherry Log, 8 miles north of Ellijay. The giveaway is the tantalizing aroma of the 'cue that saturates the mountain air. The Pink Pig is locally renowned for its tangy barbecue sauce and Brunswick stew—loaded with meat and vegetables in a tangy tomato-based sauce—but its trademark dish is fresh garlic salad. As owner Bud Holloway is fond of saying, "When you get back to Ellijay, people won't need to ask where you had lunch." Jimmy and Rosalynn Carter 'cue up at Holloway's while staying at their mountain home outside Ellijay.

To sleep off all this great eating, stop for the night at the **Home of Gardener Fatness,** a spiffy bed-and-breakfast near the square, with two rooms in the main house (built in 1910) and two others in a separate cottage. It's named for co-owner Susan

Hough's imaginary childhood friend. Each room has a different decorative theme. The Wild West Room displays an eclectic exhibit of peace officer paraphernalia collected by co-owner Walt Potter, a former north California lawman. Bring your fishing gear and you can walk down to the Ellijay River and maybe snag a couple of nice rainbow trout before breakfast. Otherwise, a big country breakfast comes with the nightly rate of $55 single, $65 double, with shared bath. Rooms are $10 additional during Apple Festival. Home of Gardener Fatness is at 59 River Street, Ellijay 30540, (706) 276–7473.

Whitewater rafters, canoeists, and kayakers flock to the Ellijay and Cartecay Rivers that flow out of the mountains, right into Ellijay. Contact Mountaintown Outdoor Expeditions, (706) 635–2524; Beacon Sports Center, (706) 276–3660; and the Gilmer County Chamber of Commerce, 5 Westside Square, Ellijay 30540, (706) 635–7400.

MIDDLE GEORGIA

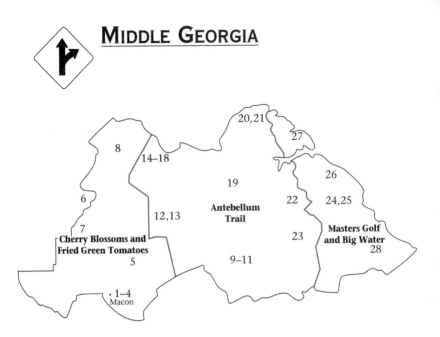

1. Downtown Macon Historic District
2. Hay House/Old Cannonball House
3. The Tubman African American Museum
4. Ocmulgee National Monument/Georgia Music Hall of Fame
5. Jarrell Plantation/Piedmont National Wildlife Refuge/Whistle Stop Café
6. Indian Springs State Park
7. High Falls State Park
8. Social Circle/Blue Willow Inn Restaurant
9. Old Governors Mansion
10. Flannery O'Connor Room
11. Milledgeville Trolley Tour/Milledgeville Ghost Walk
12. The Uncle Remus Museum
13. Rock Eagle
14. Madison–Morgan County Cultural Center
15. Morgan County African-American Museum
16. Hard Labor Creek State Park
17. Rutledge antiques and craft stores
18. Burnt Pine Plantation
19. A. H. Stephens State Historic Park/Confederate Museum
20. Washington Historical Museum/Callaway Plantation
21. Kettle Creek Battleground
22. McDuffie County Upcountry Plantation Tour
23. Old Market House
24. Riverwalk Augusta
25. Masters Golf Tournament
26. Mistletoe State Park
27. Elijah Clark State Park
28. Boll Weevil Plantation

MIDDLE GEORGIA

CHERRY BLOSSOMS AND FRIED GREEN TOMATOES

For travelers caught in the relentless grind of interstate traffic, Macon can be a quick and refreshing retreat to a slower, easier era. Only a few minutes from the major highways, ❀ **Downtown Macon Historic District** offers a glimpse at beautifully restored Greek Revival and Victorian homes, churches, and public buildings on quiet, tree-shaded streets. Three landmark houses are open year-round. Others invite guests during the late March Cherry Blossom Festival and September Jubilee..

Your first stop should be the **Macon-Bibb County Convention and Visitors Bureau,** in Terminal Station, downtown at 200 Cherry Street, Macon 31201, (800) 768–3401 and (912) 743–3401. You can pick up free maps, brochures, information, and self-guided tours. You can also sign on for **Sidney's Historic Tours.** Named in honor of Macon's beloved poet, Sidney Lanier, the tour blends historical narrative, humor, anecdotes, and passages of Lanier's romantic poetry. It includes stops at four attractions: Hay House, Cannonball House, Lanier Cottage, and Tubman Museum. **Colonel Bond's Horsedrawn Carriage Tours** depart from the Green Jacket Restaurant across from the Terminal, (912) 749–7267.

Whether with a guide or on your own, the ❀ **Hay House** (912–742–8155) will be a highlight. Five years abuilding, the opulent Italian Renaissance palazzo was finished in April 1861 just as Macon and Georgia were marching off to the War Between the States. Behind the stately redbrick facade, the twenty-four rooms are a treasure trove of stained glass, statuary, European and American furnishings, silver and crystal, paintings, silk and damask draperies and wall coverings. Long before air-conditioning, a cleverly concealed ventilation system kept the high-ceilinged rooms surprisingly cool even on the most torrid summer days. Located at 924 Georgia Avenue, Hay House is open Monday through Saturday 10:00 A.M. to 5:00 P.M. and Sunday 1:00 to 4:00 P.M. Admission for adults is $6.00; students, $2.00; and ages 6 and under, free.

Just around the corner at 856 Mulberry Street, a white-columned Greek Revival achieved lasting notoriety when a Union shell crashed through the facade and landed in the front hallway. Walk through the ◆ **Old Cannonball House** and adjoining **Macon Confederate Museum** (912–745–5982) for a look at the stray missile, Civil War photos, artifacts, china, crystal, weapons, uniforms, and such rare treasures as Mrs. Robert E. Lee's rolling pin. It's open Tuesday through Saturday 10:30 A.M. to 4:00 P.M. and Sunday 1:30 to 4:30 P.M. Adults are $3.00; senior citizens, $2.50; students, $1.00; children 12 and under, 50 cents.

Every Georgia schoolchild learns, at least for the moment, Sidney Lanier's romantic poems "The Marshes of Glynn" and "The Song of the Chattahoochee." Poet, lawyer, linguist, and musician, Lanier was born in 1842 in the tidy Victorian cottage at 935 High Street. His desk, furnishings, and personal effects are displayed at **Lanier Cottage** (912–743–3851) Monday through Friday 9:00 A.M. to 4:00 P.M. and Saturday 9:30 A.M. to 12.30 P.M. Adults are $2.50; students, $1.00; and children 12 and under, 50 cents.

Macon's modern musical heritage includes Rock 'n' Roll Hall of Famer "Little Richard" Penniman, soul singer Otis Redding (a bridge over the Ocmulgee River is named for him), and the Allman Brothers Band. Duane Allman and fellow band member Berry Oakley—both killed in 1970s motorcycle accidents—are buried in much-visited graves at **Rose Hill Cemetery.** Maconites from all the way back to the 1830s and 600 Confederate and Union soldiers are also in the historic cemetery at 1091 Riverside Drive. Call (912) 751–9119 for information.

◆ **The Tubman African American Museum,** downtown at 340 Walnut Street, (912) 743–8544, displays paintings, sculpture, and other creative endeavors by Black American, African, and Caribbean artists and craftspeople. The **Resources Room** has available reference materials and books on Black Americans. The museum's shop sells handcrafted jewelry, paintings, posters, recordings, and books. A mural depicting contemporary Black characters features Colin Powell as a military hero. Open Monday through Friday 10:00 A.M. to 5:00 P.M.; Saturday 2:00 to 5:00 P.M. Admission is $2.00 for adults and $1.00 for children.

◆ **Ocmulgee National Monument,** a short drive from downtown, is a must-see for anyone fascinated by ancient American Indian civilization. A dozen ceremonial and burial mounds, the highest nearly 45 feet, were built by Mississippian Indians between about A.D. 900 and 1100. They were succeeded at the site by Creeks, who remained here until their forced expulsion to Oklahoma in the 1830s.

Stop first at the National Park Service Visitors Center and see a short film, artifacts unearthed from the mounds, and dioramas on the cultures that flourished here. You may climb steep wooden stairs to the flat top of the 45-foot-high **Great Temple Mound** and to the crest of the surrounding smaller mounds. You may also see them from the comfort of your car. A sound-and-light presentation brings the circular **Earthlodge** back to life, as tribal elders discuss plans for a war, the effects of a drought, and other important issues. The monument is at 1207 Emery Highway, (912) 752–8257. Hours are (daily) 9:00 A.M. to 5:00 P.M. Free admission.

The ♦ **Georgia Music Hall of Fame,** opening in spring 1996 at 305 Coliseum Drive, (912) 738–0017, promises to be one of the state's most outstanding attractions. In downtown Macon, the contemporary 42,000-square-foot museum and exhibition hall honors such legendary Macon-linked musicians as Otis Redding, Duane Allman, James Brown, "Little Richard" Penniman, Capricorn Records's Phil Walden, and Georgia-born legends such as Lena Horne, Jessye Norman, Gladys Knight, Johnny Mercer, Harry James, and Ray Charles. Displays and audiovisual presentations feature memorabilia and music of the stars, a 1950s soda fountain, Gospel Chapel, Rhythm and Blues Revue, a live performance theater, a restaurant, and a gift shop. Open daily. Admission is $6.50 for adults.

If you have time for only one meal in Macon, make it **Len Berg's,** downtown in the Post Office Alley, (912) 742–9255. A Macon landmark for many, many years, this comfortable ensemble of small rooms and comfortable booths serves first-class Southern cooking, from fried fish to fried chicken, country fried steak to pork chops, turnip greens, squash casserole and macaroni and cheese, fried okra, biscuits, corn bread, and hot cobblers. Len Berg's downtown is open for lunch Monday to Saturday. **Len Berg's Carryout,** in Ingleside Village, at Ingleside and Corbin Avenues off Riverside Drive in north Macon, (912) 743–7011, serves the original's same delicious food to take home or enjoy in dine-in booths. Lunch and dinner are served Monday to Saturday. Upscale Ingleside Village has many gift, antiques, art, apparel, and ice-cream shops under its brightly colored awnings.

Nathalia's, at 2720 Riverside Drive, (912) 741–1380, has satisfied Macon's hunger for classical Italian cooking since 1984. Grilled veal chops, risotto, osso buco, pasta, seafood, and chicken dishes are complemented by light delicate sauces. (No red sauces or meatballs.) There is also a wide selection of Italian, French, and American wines by the bottle and glass. Dinner is served Monday to Saturday.

For another taste of Macon, try the plump, juicy hot dogs loaded with chili and other toppings at **Nu-Way Wieners,** a hometown chain with a downtown outlet at Cherry Street and Cotton Avenue, (912) 743–1368.

To get in the proper antebellum spirit, make reservations at the **1842 Inn,** 353 College Street, Macon 31201, (912) 741–1842. The twenty-two guest rooms in the circa 1842 Greek Revival showplace are decorated with antiques, fresh flowers, fireplaces, and all the contemporary comforts. Double rates of $95 to $145 include continental breakfast.

During the last ten days of March, more than 200,000 Japanese cherry trees set the stage for the city's annual **Cherry Blossom Festival** highlighted by concerts, home and garden tours, parades, and other activities. You won't be in town very long before proud Maconites tell you that in sheer numbers of blossoming trees, if nothing else, their festival is bigger than Washington, D.C.'s.

Cherry Blossom season or not, you'll still enjoy a drive by the stately homes on north Macon's **"Cherry Blossom Trail,"** several miles of streets marked by pink and white signs. Stop for a light lunch at the **Sassafras Tearoom** in Ocmulgee Center, 2242 Ingleside Avenue, (912) 746–3336. There's a selection of collectibles in the back and the first-class **Ocmulgee Arts Gallery** and **Picket Fence** women's wear shop are next door. **Jim Shaw's,** 3040 Vineville Avenue, (912) 746–3697, is a popular north Macon destination for mesquite grilled and blackened fish and fried and broiled shrimp and scallops, steak, and alligator.

◆**Jarrell Plantation** is a homespun juxtaposition to the romanticized Old South of Tara and Twelve Oaks, dashing beaux and ladies fair. At the end of a tree-shaded graveled road off Highway 18 between Forsyth and Gray, you enter a world where unrelenting hard work—not flirtation and idle mint juleps—was the rule of society. From the early 1840s, when John Fitz Jarrell built the first dwelling, until 1958 when the last direct heir died, the plantation was worked by three generations of Jarrells. They planted cotton, ran gins and gristmills, and battled boll weevils, depressions, and General William Tecumseh Sherman himself. Nowadays, the dwellings, work buildings, barnyards, and fields are maintained by the Georgia Department of Natural Resources as a living memorial to the state's agricultural heritage.

You'll enter the plantation through the scuppernong arbor, whose juicy fruit Jarrell women turned into pies and jellies. A flock of guinea fowl, squawking like so many feathered burglar alarms, alerted the family that visitors were approaching. These days, the guinea fowl still sound off, and an assortment of barnyard animals—a goat, a horse, a brown milk cow, a burro, a couple of sheep—press against the fence for the hay held out by children.

At the modern new visitors center, you can watch a film on the plantation's history and pick up a self-guided walking tour map.

At the 1847 plantation's plain first dwelling, you can visualize the womenfolk sitting in a circle, their hands busily making quilts and clothes while hearty stews bubbled on the wood-burning stove. At the mill complex down the hill from the house, workmen get the steam engine ready to grind the sugar cane into syrup.

Jarrell Plantation—Route 1, Box 40, Juliette 31046, (912) 986-5172—is open Tuesday through Saturday 9:00 A.M. to 5:00 P.M. and Sunday 2:00 to 5:00 P.M. Adults are $2.00; children 6 to 18, $1.00; 5 and under, free..

The ◆ **Piedmont National Wildlife Refuge,** 10 miles down the graveled road from the plantation, has a visitors center and hiking trails. You can bring your fishing gear and try your luck in the Ocmulgee River.

If you saw the movie *Fried Green Tomatoes* or read the Fannie Flagg novel it was based on, you'll be glad to know it wasn't pure fiction. After the movie's highly successful 1991 run, enterprising folks in the almost-ghost town of **Juliette** bought up the store that served as the movie's café and reopened the "new" ◆ **Whistle Stop Café,** (912) 994-3670. Fried green tomatoes are served, along with barbecue, fried chicken, meat loaf, pork chops, and other home-cooked favorites. Southern-style breakfast is also served. The block of stores and the white frame depot around the cafe have also been revived as antiques and gift shops. And, adding to the atmosphere, local kids dive off the dam near the textile mill, just as they did in the film. The Whistle Stop Café is open daily. It's in downtown Juliette, 10 miles off I-75 north and south exit 61.

A quiet and peaceful recreation place now, ◆ **Indian Springs State Park,** near Jackson, has a long, colorful, and tragic history. For many centuries Creeks and other Indians gathered at a sulfur spring whose waters were believed to have magical powers to cure ailments and restore vitality. In the spring in 1825, Creek Indian Chief William McIntosh signed an illegal treaty ceding all tribal lands to the state of Georgia. The fraudulent treaty so enraged the dispossessed Indians that they murdered McIntosh and several of his followers. A valid treaty in 1828 finally ended Creek dominion. The town of Indian Springs was founded, along with what's believed to be the oldest state park anywhere in the United States.

Nowadays people still flock to the sulfur springs and take home jugs of the strong-smelling water. They swear by its ability to restore health and vitality and offer this advice to those who quail at the rotten-egg smell: Just let it sit for two to three days, and the aroma will vanish, but not the curative strength of the minerals.

The handsome fieldstone buildings in the park were built during the Great Depression by the Civilian Conservation Corps. Along with the mineral waters, artifacts and historical displays are on view at the **Indian Museum.** Around a 105-acre lake are a swimming beach, fishing, rental boats, nature trails, and picnic areas. Campsites with electrical and water hookups are $10 a night. Completely furnished two-bedroom cottages, with log-burning fireplaces, are available. There is a $2.00 per visit parking fee. Contact Park Superintendent, Indian Springs 30231, (770) 504–2277. For reservations call (800) 864–PARK.

Fresh Air Bar-B-Que (770–775–3182), on Highway 23 between Jackson and the park, is one of the holy grails of this savory Georgia art form. Except for wooden planking that covered the old sawdust floor a few years ago, and one change of ownership nearly fifty years ago, this rambling, wooden barbecue shack has changed only marginally since it served its first platter in 1929.

The pine board tables have been in place for more than forty years. Pork is slowly cooked over hickory and oak coals right behind the ordering counter. It's sweet and succulent, with a tangy pièce de résistance provided by a secret sauce prepared every day by G. W. "Toots" Caston, the patriarch of the family that has operated the place since the early 1940s. Along with barbecued pork, the simple menu includes only Brunswick stew, cole slaw, slabs of starchy white bread, soft drinks, and iced tea. It's open Monday through Thursday 7:00 A.M. to 7:30 P.M., Friday and Saturday until 9:30 P.M., and on Sunday until 8:30 P.M.. During the summer, it usually remains open a half hour to an hour later.

◆**High Falls State Park,** off Highway 36, about 12 miles south of Indian Springs, is another rustic off-the-beaten-path retreat. The centerpiece is a series of scenic whitewater cataracts of the **Towaliga River** rushing over mossy rocks. According to legend, Creek Indians "cured" their victims' scalps around the Towaliga—hence the name, which means "roasted scalp."

Two hiking trails offer views of the falls, the river, and adjacent woodlands. You can wade into the river but be extremely careful of the slick, mossy rocks. Also in the 995-acre park, you'll find a 650-acre lake for fishing and boating, a swimming pool, and 142 tent and trailer sites, with water and electrical hookups. There is a $2.00 per visit parking fee. Contact Park Superintendent, Route 5, Box 108, Jackson 30233, (912) 994–5080. For reservations call (800) 864–PARK.

The little Walton County town of ◆**Social Circle,** about 8 miles west of Hard Labor Creek on Highway 11, is a delightful place to stroll and browse. The nineteenth-century storefronts have been brightly repainted, and three are antiques shops. The wooden shelves in Claude Wiley's Store are stacked to the ceiling with canned goods, overalls, farm products, and household necessities. The town allegedly got its name when a stranger happened onto a cluster of idling locals and found them so friendly he proclaimed, "Why, this is sure some social circle."

The ◆**Blue Willow Inn Restaurant** (770–454–2131) is like an old-fashioned Sunday dinner at grandma's. The dining room of the 1890s Victorian house is filled with a bountiful buffet that includes fried chicken, pork chops, chicken and dumplings, baked ham, an array of vegetables (including state-of-the-art fried green tomatoes), congealed salads, cake, and fruit cobbler—all at astonishingly modest prices. Open daily.

Lake Oconee, a mammoth Georgia Power Company impoundment of the Oconee River, is a major destination for outdoor recreation. The 19,000-acre lake, with a 375-mile shoreline, has numerous marinas, campsites, picnicking areas, and swimming beaches. The Georgia Power Company office at the lake (800–886–LAKE) can supply further information about recreational facilities. The lake is easily accessible from I–20.

Three country club and golf communities on Lake Oconee welcome overnight guests in cottages and villas. Guests enjoy championship-style golf courses, lighted tennis courts, fitness centers, swimming pools, croquet, horseback riding, marinas, dining, and other first-class facilities. Contact **Harbor Club,** One Club Drive, Greensboro 30642, (770) 453–4414; **Port Armor,** One Port Armor Parkway, Greensboro 30642, (770) 453–4561; and **Reynolds Plantation,** 100 Linger Longer Road, Greensboro 30642, (770) 467–3151.

ANTEBELLUM TRAIL

Milledgeville was Georgia's capital city from early after the Revolution until after the War Between the States. Laid out in 1803–1804 on a precise grid of broad streets and public squares, it was the only American city other than Washington, D.C., specifically planned as a capital. In its own way, it was to post-Revolutionary Georgia what Brasilia was to mid-twentieth-century Brazil: a magnet intended to lure settlers away from the comforts of the Atlantic coast.

Statesmen and public officials eased the burdens of the wilderness by building palatial Greek Revival mansions filled with the finest American and European furnishings, books, and art. Halcyon days ended in the fall of 1864 when General William T. Sherman's Union army, marching from Atlanta to Savannah, captured the city.

According to which legend you choose to believe, Milledgeville was spared Sherman's torch because (a) he was met at the outskirts by fellow brothers of the local Masonic lodge, who pleaded for leniency; (b) he didn't want to burn a town he'd chosen as temporary headquarters; (c) he had a local lady friend and did not wish to break her heart.

Whatever the reasons, Milledgeville's peaceable surrender was accomplished when Governor Joseph E. Brown stood in the rotunda of the Governors Mansion and handed his sword to General Sherman. When the "March to the Sea" resumed, the Governors Mansion and everything of nonmilitary importance was left unharmed. The Reconstruction government moved the capital to Atlanta, an action ratified by the state's voters in 1868.

Built in 1835 to 1838 in Palladian design Greek Revival style, the ◆ **Old Governors Mansion** (912–453–4545) has been beautifully restored and refurnished. Guided tours of public rooms rich with original furnishings and fascinating architectural features are conducted Tuesday through Saturday 10:00 A.M. to 4:00 P.M. and Sunday 2:00 to 5:00 P.M. Adults are $3.00; students, $1.00. It's in the center of the town at 120 South Clark Street.

American literature fans should also visit the ◆ **Flannery O'Connor Room** (912–453–5573) in the library of neighboring Georgia College. The late author wrote her two novels *(The Violent Bear It Away* and *Wise Blood)* and short story collections while living here. She died in 1964 and is buried in Memory Hill Cemetery. The Flannery O'Connor Room at her alma mater displays first editions, manuscripts, gifts from admirers, memorabilia, and drawings she did as a hobby. It's open Monday through Friday 8:00 A.M. to 5:00 P.M.

The best way to enjoy the town's heritage is on a two-hour motorized ◆ **Milledgeville Trolley Tour,** which covers the major landmarks and includes a visit to the Governors Mansion. Guides weave a wealth of humor and anecdotes into their historical narrative. Tours leave the Milledgeville Convention and Visitors Bureau, 200 West Hancock Street, Milledgeville 31061, Tuesdays and Fridays at 10:00 A.M. Adults are $8.50, $3.25 ages 6 to 12. The tourism office (912–452–4687 and 800–653–1804) also has free maps and information for self-guided walking tours. It's directly across the street from the handsome **Baldwin County Courthouse.**

Milledgeville is a "high-spirited" town. If you'd like to hear about some of its specters, join the ◆ **Milledgeville Ghost Walk.** The hour-and-a half stroll through the historic district begins at dusk Wednesday through Saturday, and you never know who (or what) you'll encounter along the way. Adults are $6.50; ages 6 to 12, $4.50. Call beeper phone (800) 484–1087 extension 6405 or (706) 485–0741.

For dinner Tuesday through Sunday, try the crisply fried catfish and hushpuppies, shrimp, and other fresh seafood at **Chobys Landing** (912–453–9744), 3090 Highway 441 north, and **Totten's Fisherman's Wharf** (912–452–0161), 170 Sinclair Marina Road. Both are on **Lake Sinclair,** north of town, with docking facilities near the door.

Two historic Milledgeville homes invite bed-and-breakfast guests: **Mara's Tara,** 330 West Greene Street, Milledgeville 31061, (912) 453–2732; and **Hinson House,** 200 North Columbia Street, Milledgeville 31061, (912) 452–4687. Both have beautiful antique furnishings, private baths, and breakfast for about $60 a double.

After Milledgeville's history lesson, you'll probably be ready for some quiet relaxation. Lake Sinclair, a 15,330-acre, 420-mile shoreline impoundment of the Oconee River, has plenty of stretching room. Marinas, fishing docks, and campgrounds are off U.S. Highway 441 north of Milledgeville.

Milledgeville's literary lioness was Flannery O'Connor. Eatonton, about 15 miles north on U.S. 441, was the birthplace in 1848 of Joel Chandler Harris, who turned the slave legends he heard as a youngster on a Putnam County plantation into "The Uncle Remus Tales."

❖ **The Uncle Remus Museum** (706–485–6856), on Highway 441 south of the town of 4,800 has Harris's personal mementos and illustrations of the tales of the devilish Br'er Rabbit, sly-but-perpetually-outwitted Br'er Fox, dumb ole Br'er Bear, and, of course, the Tar Baby. Also in the log cabin, which was created from two original slave cabins, you'll see first editions, a diorama of an antebellum plantation, and other historical artifacts. The museum is open daily during the summer 9:00 A.M. to 5:00 P.M. and closed on Tuesday the rest of the year. Adults are $1.00; children, 50 cents.

As you drive past the Putnam County Courthouse in the center of Eatonton, look for the little likeness of Br'er Rabbit on the lawn facing Highway 441. Many well-kept antebellum homes are on the shady streets leading off the courthouse square. Putnam County is also the center of Georgia's dairy industry, so you'll also spot several contented herds as you drive out of town.

❖ **Rock Eagle,** 4 miles north of Eatonton, is a relic of Indian civilizations that flourished here more than 6,000 years ago. A creamy white quartz effigy—about 10 feet high, 103 feet from its head to its tail, 32 feet from wingtip to wingtip—the great bird seems poised for flight. Archaeologists believe Rock Eagle was a focus for Indian tribal rituals. The best views are from an observation tower. It's located in a 4-H Club Center, on Highway 74, off Highway 441.

Morgan County, between Augusta and Atlanta, claims Madison, one of Georgia's prettiest antebellum towns. Before leaving, you can relax at a state park with an 18-hole golf course, fish and swim at a 19,000-acre lake, and hunt quail on a private preserve.

Strolling along the tree-shaded streets and picturesque town square, admiring Madison's treasury of glorious antebellum architecture, we should say "thank you" to a United States senator who put himself between the town and General William T. Sherman's torch. In late 1864, Atlanta in ruins 60 miles away and the cruel "March to the Sea" in full stride, Sherman's Union army approached Madison's outskirts. They were met by former Senator Joshua Hill, a foe of secession who'd been acquainted with Sherman in Washington. He peacefully surrendered the town, which was miraculously spared war's ravages.

Your first stop should be the **Madison–Morgan County Chamber of Commerce Welcome Center,** 115 East Jefferson Street, Madison 30650, (706) 342–3207. In this former 1880s fire station on the courthouse square, you can load up on walking-tour maps and brochures and get any information you may need on festivals, bed-and-breakfasts, and restaurants. Stop next at the ◆ **Madison–Morgan County Cultural Center,** 434 South Main Street, Madison 30650, (706) 342–4743. The Romanesque-style redbrick schoolhouse, circa 1895, is now the hub for regional arts, theater performances, and the source of walking-tour maps of the fetching little town of 3,000. The former schoolrooms now show pottery, weaving, paintings by Georgia artists and traveling exhibitions, nineteenth-century furniture, farm implements, clothing, and Civil War artifacts. You may also see a log cabin from the early 1800s and an 1890s schoolroom, complete with pot-bellied stove and hickory switch. The center's August theater festival features everything from Shakespeare to Tennessee Williams. The center is open Tuesday through Saturday 10:00 A.M. to 4:30 P.M. and Sunday 2:00 to 5:00 P.M. Admission is $2.50 adults; students, $1.50; no charge on Wednesday.

With a self-guided tour map, walk through the **Madison National Historic District** and admire more than three-dozen gorgeous Greek Revival, Neoclassical, Victorian, Federal, and Romanesque homes, many of them graced by gardens and stately trees. A number of these old beauties are open to the public during Madison's May and December festivals.

The ◆ **Morgan County African American Museum,** 156

Academy Street, (706) 342–9191, documents the contributions Blacks have made to the area's cultural and social life. Located in the 1895 Horace Moore House, the museum has rooms with period furnishings, a reference library, paintings, books, and exhibits. Open Tuesday to Saturday. Adults are $2.00; children, $1.00.

You may take a guided tour of **Heritage Hall,** 277 South Main Street, (706) 342–9627, a white-columned 1830s Greek Revival showplace near the courthouse square. Look for romantic messages etched on the windows, and be mindful of a mysterious presence that sometimes evidences itself in an upstairs bedroom. Open daily. Adults are $2.50; seniors, $2.00; students, $1.00.

Madison's town square is one of Georgia's most delightful, and the **Morgan County Courthouse** one of the grandest of the 159 counties. Several antiques and handicraft stores will draw your attention as you stroll around the square. When hunger strikes, head for the cafeteria line at **Ye Old Colonial** (706–342–2211), a unique dining landmark on the square. Once upon a time the building was a bank, which accounts for the high ceilings, tiled floors, and a small dining room in the one-time vault. These days you can cash in on excellent fried chicken, barbecue, fish, Southern-style vegetables, and hearty breakfasts with biscuits and buttery grits. Service is continuous from breakfast through lunch and dinner Monday through Saturday.

Two of Madison's loveliest homes welcome bed-and-breakfast guests: **Brady Inn,** 250 North Second Street, (706) 342–4400; and **Burnett Place,** 317 Old Post Road, (706) 342–4034. Both are in zip code 30650.

◆ **Hard Labor Creek State Park,** 12 miles west of Madison, near the small community of Rutledge, is a nice place to relax for a day, or several days. The recreational possibilities include a very good 18-hole golf course and a lake for swimming, boating, and fishing. Plenty of picnic tables are spread among the pines, and there's a playground for the youngsters. If you're planning to play the 6,682-yard, par-72 course, bring your own clubs. You may rent an electric cart in the clubhouse, which has showers and a snack bar. The park's fifty campsites have water, electricity, rest rooms, and showers; twenty two-bedroom cottages are completely furnished, including towels, sheets, and kitchen utensils. There is a $2.00 per visit parking fee. The park office is open daily 8:00 A.M. to 5:00 P.M. Contact Superintendent, Rutledge 30663, (706)

557–3001. For reservations call (800) 864–PARK.

Until recently Rutledge was a couple of blinks you passed through on the way to Hard Labor Creek. During the past few years, a group of citizens has bought up much of the town of 650 and attracted a cadre of artists and craftspeople from as far away as New England. ◆ **Rutledge antiques and craft stores** on the main street sell handmade quilts, handcrafted furniture, original art work, pottery, and antiques. Have lunch or dinner at **The Yesterday Cafe,** (706) 557–9337, a handsomely redone turn-of-the-century drug store with bare brick walls and a tiled floor, which blends Southern cooking with trendy pasta, veal, beef, and chicken dishes. It's open daily for breakfast and lunch and dinner Thursday through Saturday. Take the Rutledge/Hard Labor Creek exit from I–20.

◆ **Burnt Pine Plantation,** a 10,000-acre spread of fields, woodlands, and hedgerows near Madison, is a private preserve dedicated to the sport of quail and dove hunting. Guests are furnished with guides and dogs. Accommodations and meals are at a comfortable lodge and adjacent, fully furnished cottages. Contact Burnt Pine Plantation, 2941 Little River Road, Madison 30650, (706) 342–7202.

Two miles off I–20 exit 55, drowsy little Crawfordville is small-town America of a long-gone yesteryear. Guarded by a granite Johnny Reb, the redbrick Taliaferro ("Tolliver" in the English fashion) County Courthouse presides over a quiet square, where old gentlemen sit and gossip under sidewalk arcades. Tranquil as it is, Crawfordville has significant historic and culinary treasures.

In her cheery cafe across from the courthouse, Mrs. Annie Lou Bonner has created state-of-the-art sweet potato pie and other stars of the Southern galaxy since 1926 at Mrs. Bonner's Cafe (706–456–2347). Deep burnt-orange in hue, fragrant with ginger, cinnamon, and nutmeg, the creamy sweet potato filling rests atop a thin, flaky crust that Mrs. Bonner prepares from scratch every morning. Before the pie have a plate of her fried chicken, baked ham, barbecue, or pork chops, with fresh vegetables and corn bread and a large glass of sweetened iced tea, and for less than $5.00, you've taken a long look into the Southern soul. She's on hand from early morning to late at night Monday through Saturday.

Two blocks from Mrs. Bonner's Cafe, ◆ **A. H. Stephens**

A. H. Stephens State Historic Park

State Historic Park includes the home and gravesite of Alexander Hamilton Stephens, governor of Georgia and vice-president of the Confederacy. **Liberty Hall,** the two-story frame house Stephens built around 1830, is filled with his furnishings, personal effects, and the wheelchairs to which he was bound much of his life.

The adjoining ❖**Confederate Museum** (706–456–2602) is highlighted by a bronze statue of Stephens by Gutzon Borglum, sculptor of the U.S. presidents on Mount Rushmore, South Dakota. This fine collection of memorabilia also includes dioramas of soldiers in the heat of battle and the quiet of the campfire; rifles and shot; field gear; battle flags; and touching personal belongings—Bibles, prayer books, and bloodstained photos of wives and sweethearts.

As in all wars, Civil War soldiers used sharp-edged humor to help blunt the insidious enemies of fear and homesickness. "In this army," a Confederate foot soldier wrote, "one hole in the seat of the breeches indicates a captain, two holes is for a lieutenant, and the seat of the pants all out is for us privates." Liberty Hall and the Confederate Museum are open Monday and Wednesday through Saturday 9:00 A.M. to 5:00 P.M. and Sunday 2:00 to 5:30 P.M. Closed Tuesday. Adults are $2.00; ages 5 to 18, $1.00; under age 5, no charge.

After your history lesson, relax at the park's recreation area. A quarter-mile from Liberty Hall, you'll find a swimming pool, two fishing lakes, picnic shelters, and thirty-six tent and trailer sites, with water and electrical hookups, showers, and rest rooms. For reservations call (800) 864–PARK. There is a $2.00 per visit parking fee.

Incorporated in 1780, the picture book little town of Washington was the first American community named in honor of the father of our country. Skirted by General William T. Sherman's rampaging "March to the Sea" and treated kindly by progress and time, the town of about 5,000 is today like a living Williamsburg. More than thirty Greek Revival homes, churches, and public buildings predate 1850. Most of them are still well-maintained residences. Three antebellum landmarks are open to visitors year-round.

The **Robert Toombs House State Historic Site,** 216 East Robert Toombs Avenue, (706) 678–2226, was the home of Georgia's "Unreconstructed Rebel," U.S. senator, and Confederate secretary of state. At odds with the Confederacy—he was resentful of Jefferson Davis's presidency—as well as the Union, he fled to the Caribbean and Europe after the war. Returning in 1880, he scorned political pardon. "I am not loyal to the government of the United States," he declared, "and do not wish to be suspected of loyalty." The guided tours of his Greek Revival house include a documentary film, anecdotes, historical exhibits, and several rooms with period furnishings. Open Wednesday through Saturday 9:00 A.M. to 5:00 P.M. and Sunday 2:00 to 5:30 P.M. Adults are $2.00; ages 18 and under, $1.00; under age 5, no charge.

The ◆ **Washington Historical Museum,** 308 East Robert Toombs Avenue, (706) 678–2105, houses an outstanding collection of Civil War artifacts including Jefferson Davis's camp chest (given to him by English sympathizers), weapons, uniforms, signed documents, photographs, and furnishings. The main floor of the circa 1835–1836 two-story frame house is furnished as a typical nineteenth-century double parlor, dining room, and bedroom. The ground floor has been restored as a period kitchen. The grounds are noted for beautiful landscaping and one of Georgia's largest camellia gardens. Hours are Tuesday through Saturday 10:00 A.M. to 5:00 P.M. and Sunday 2:00 to 5:00 P.M. Adult admission is $1.50; ages 12 to 18, $1.00; children 6 to 12, 75 cents.

◆ **Callaway Plantation,** 5 miles west of Washington on Highway 78, (706) 678–7060, is a living heritage museum rich in lessons about Southern antebellum life. Three restored homes and the adjoining farm are like a walk back in time. The redbrick, white-columned manor house was the heart of a 3,000-acre cotton plantation. Rooms are furnished with period antiques and many unique architectural features. The outbuildings include a hewn log cabin, circa 1785, with early domestic and agricultural tools and primitive furniture and a smokehouse, barn, pigeon house, and cemetery. Surrounding fields are planted with cotton, corn, cane, and vegetables, just as they were in the mid-nineteenth century. The plantation has been owned by the same family since the late eighteenth century, and it's open Tuesday through Sunday 10:00 A.M. to 5:00 P.M. Adults are $2.00; ages 12 to 18, $1.50; children ages 6 to 12, $1.00.

Washington also figured in the Revolutionary War. A marker at ◆ **Kettle Creek Battleground,** 8 miles south of town on Highway 44, commemorates the patriots' 1779 rout of the British and the Redcoats' subsequent withdrawal from this area of Georgia. Picnic tables are at the site.

When hunger overwhelms your hunt through history, head for **Another Thyme** (706–678–1672), an attractive cafe in the lobby of the Victorian Fitzpatrick Hotel on the courthouse square. Midday fare includes sandwiches, soups, salads, plate lunches, and homemade desserts Monday through Saturday and dinner Monday through Saturday.

Sleep in the bower of history at any of these Washington-area bed-and-breakfasts: **The Belle Sterling,** 412 East Robert Toombs Avenue, Washington 30673, (706) 678–5388; **Wingfield,** 512 North Alexander Avenue, Washington 30673, (706) 678–2278; **Four Chimneys,** 2316 Wire Road, Thomson 30824, (706) 597–0220; **1810 West Inn,** 254 North Seymour Drive, Thomson 30824, (706) 595–3156 and (800) 515–1810; and **Davis House Inn,** 106 Laurel Avenue, Greensboro 30642, (706) 453–4213.

Many of Washington's most magnificent homes are open during the early April **Washington-Wilkes Tour of Homes.** Contact Washington-Wilkes Chamber of Commerce, P.O. Box 661, Washington 30673, (706) 678–2013.

If your group numbers at least ten, you can take a trip through history on the ◆ **McDuffie County Upcountry Plantation Tour.** You'll set out from the Thomson–McDuffie County Tourism Bureau in the restored train depot and stop at the **Rock House,** a 1785 fieldstone farmhouse; **Alexandria,** a stately Virginia-influenced brick plantation house and boxwood gardens from 1805; and the site of November's **Belle Meade Fox Hunt.** A number of gracious antebellum homes line Thomson's tree-shaded streets. Contact Thomson-McDuffie County Tourism Bureau, 111 Railroad Street, Thomson 30824, (706) 595–5584. You can stay overnight at the **1810 West Inn,** built sometime around that year. Guest rooms have antiques and private baths. Contact 1810 West Inn, 254 North Seymour Drive, Thomson 30824, (706) 595–3156.

The ◆ **Old Market House** is a souvenir of the period from 1796 to 1805 when little Louisville ("Lewis-ville") was Georgia's capital. Built in the 1790s, the Market's weathered timbers are held together by 1-inch-diameter wooden pegs. The Market's bell was cast in France in 1722 and was on its way to a New Orleans convent when it was hijacked by pirates and somehow ended up in Louisville. Louisville's tenure as state capital was immortalized by the Great Yazoo Land Fraud of 1795, which cost Georgia the territory that later became the states of Alabama and Mississippi.

Wind up your sightseeing with some historic Southern cooking at **Pansy's Restaurant** on Louisville's main street, (912) 625–3216.

MASTERS GOLF AND BIG WATER

Augusta, a city of 45,000 with 450,000 in the metropolitan area, traces its heritage back to 1736, when General James Edward Oglethorpe, father of the Georgia Crown Colony, laid it out as the state's second city, after Savannah. Fought for during the Revolutionary War and skirted by General William T. Sherman's "March to the Sea," Augusta has mild winters and a genteel Old Southern lifestyle that caught the attention of post–Civil War Northern aristocrats, who found the right formula for golf—a pastime that symbolizes this city to sportsmen around the world.

For many years Augusta almost forgot that the Savannah River ran by its doorstep. All that is changing rapidly as ◆ **Riverwalk Augusta** becomes a new center of downtown activity. The main entrance to Riverwalk is at Eighth and Reynolds Streets, a block off Broad Street. The top of the old river levee has been turned into an inviting brick esplanade with seating clusters overlooking the river, historical displays, and playground and picnic areas. Major hotels, shops, and dining are along the Riverwalk. Stop first at the Cotton Exchange Welcome Center, Eighth and Reynolds Streets, for information and historic exhibits on Augusta's once-lucrative trade in "white gold." It's open Monday through Saturday 9:00 A.M. to 5:00 P.M. and Sunday 1:00 to 5:00 P.M. Phone (706) 724–4067 or (800) 726–0243. Self-guided walking and driving tours as well as group tours are available at the welcome center.

The **Augusta-Richmond County Museum** is now part of Riverwalk's excitement. Early in 1996 the sixty-year-old "municipal attic" moved into a new 48,000-square-foot home at Sixth and Reynolds Streets. The twenty-three permanent galleries are filled with Revolutionary and Civil War weapons and uniforms, Native American culture, natural history (including a major dinosaur exhibit), space exploration, communications, vintage photographs, and a tribute to the city's and Georgia's founding father, Gen. James Edward Oglethorpe. Savannah River marine life inhabits a small aquarium. Train buffs shouldn't miss "Old

101

No. 302," the Georgia Railroad's last steam engine. Open Tuesday to Saturday 10:00 A.M. to 6:00 P.M., Sunday 2:00 to 5:00 P.M. Adults are $4.00; children and seniors, $2.00. Phone (706) 722–8454.

The Riverwalk is slated to be the home of two other new museums in 1996 and 1997. The **National Science Center,** a hands-on math and science museum for inquiring minds of all ages, will have a high-tech theater and scores of interactive exhibits on electronics, computer arts, and communications. Scheduled to open in spring 1996, the two-story, 128,000-square-foot museum is a joint venture of the U.S. Army and NSC Discovery, Inc., a nonprofit scientific organization. Contact the Augusta-Richmond County Convention and Visitors Bureau for more information.

The **Georgia Golf Hall of Fame** will pay tribute to the game that has so many proud roots in Augusta and elsewhere in the state. A museum will honor legendary grand-slammer Bobby Jones and thirty other members of the Georgia Golf Hall of Fame. An interactive theater will let golfers challenge some of the world's most renowned courses. It's scheduled to open in early 1997.

You can stay in the heart of the Riverwalk at the **Radisson Riverfront Hotel,** 2 Tenth Street, Augusta 30901, (706) 722–8900. The modern 234-room hotel has full-service dining, entertainment, health club, and many other amenities. Rates run about $100 for a double.

Sacred Heart Cultural Center, 1301 Greene Street, (706) 826–4700, is a heartening and very spectacular example of a cherished piece of architectural heritage, down on its luck, given a new lease on life. Consecrated in 1901, the redbrick, twin-spired Romanesque Catholic church summed up the highest skills of European artists. Jewel-like tones of German stained-glass windows played against the creamy white Italian marble columns, stations of the cross, and the ornate high altar. In the early 1970s, with much of its congregation now in the subrbs, Sacred Heart's doors were closed, the church deconsecrated and left to the mercy of the elements and vandals.

The church would probably have kept a date with the wrecking ball if an "angel" in the form of an affluent and civic-minded corporate executive hadn't come to the rescue. Following an extensive renovation, Sacred Heart Cultural Center is now the scene of banquets, wedding receptions, fashion shows, chamber concerts, and numerous other functions. A gift shop on the lower floor sells works by local artists and authors. You may take a self-guided tour of the sanctuary Monday through Friday between 8:30 A.M. and 5:30 P.M.; donations are accepted. Guided tours are by appointment 1:00 to 4:00 P.M. Adults are $2.00; senior citizens and students, $1.00.

Ezekiel Harris House, 1840 Broad Street, (706) 724–0436, is Augusta's second-oldest structure. In 1797 Harris came to the area from South Carolina with plans to build a town to rival Augusta as a tobacco market. On a hill overlooking Augusta, the house is an outstanding example of post-Revolutionary architecture. The gambrel roof and vaulted hallway are reminiscent of New England. Tiered piazzas are supported by artistically beveled wooden posts. Rooms are furnished with period antiques. It's open Monday through Friday 1:00 to 4:00 P.M. and Saturday 10:00 A.M. to 4:00 P.M. Adults are $2.00; students, 50 cents.

Meadow Garden, Independence Drive near the intersection of Walton Way and Thirteenth Street, (706) 724–4174, was the home of George Walton, one of Georgia's signers of the Declaration of Independence. Built around 1791, it's the city's oldest documented structure and has been restored and refurnished by the Georgia Society, Daughters of the American Revolution. Hours are Monday through Friday 9:00 A.M. to 4:00 P.M., Saturday 10:00 A.M. to 4:00 P.M., Sunday 1:00 to 4:00 P.M. Admission for adults is $2.00 and 50 cents for children.

La Maison, in a restored mansion in the Old Town Historic District at 404 Telfair Street, (706) 722–4805, prepares the city's most sophisticated cuisine. Former Atlanta chef Heinz Sowinski's repertoire includes a wide range of French, German, Swiss, and other specialties. For adventurous tastes, the "Game Sampler" is a platter of three or four exotic, richly sauced meat dishes such as pheasant, smoked venison, quail, or wild boar. Magnificent desserts reflect Sowinski's European culinary heritage. Cocktails and a large selection of American, Australian, and European wines round out the menu. Dinner is served Monday through Saturday.

Gertrude Herbert Institute of Art, 506 Telfair Street, (706) 722–5495, is an architecturally outstanding early–nineteenth-century residence that showcases regional and Southeastern contemporary art. Built in 1818 by Augusta Mayor Nicholas Ware, the elliptical three-story staircase, Adam-style mantels, and other rich ornamentation earned it the name

"Ware's Folly." Hours are Tuesday through Friday 10:00 A.M. to 5:00 P.M. and Saturday 10:00 A.M. to 2:00 P.M. Admission for adults is $2.00; children and seniors, $1.00.

The **Town Tavern,** 15 Seventh Street at the Riverwalk, (706) 724–1030, recently celebrated its fifty-fifth anniversary. The American menu includes seafood, steaks, salads, and full Southern breakfast in an attractive Early American motif. It's open for lunch and dinner Monday through Saturday. Credit cards are accepted, and prices are moderate.

If you're into antiquing, head for the 1200 block of Broad Street, where you'll find an extensive cluster of shops and flea markets.

Kids and kids at heart shouldn't miss **Fat Man's Forest** (706–722–0796). A rambling array of added-on buildings at 1545 Laney-Walker Boulevard, Fat Man's is locally renowned for its holiday paraphernalia. At Halloween people come from miles around to rent costumes, purchase pumpkins and made-to-order jack-o'-lanterns, and send their youngsters through the haunted house. At Christmas the kids ride a festive train while grownups browse for trees, gifts, and decorations. Whatever the season it's a fun place to wander and marvel at the Fat Man's ingenuity.

For golfers around the globe, Augusta is Christmas, the World Series, the rainbow's end. In late March and early April, fortunate faithful congregate along the dogwood- and azalea-rimmed fairways of storied **Augusta National Golf Club** to hail the game's elite as they pursue the Green Jacket, symbolic of the ◆ **Masters Golf Tournament** championship. Unless you know a player or a club member, tickets to the championship rounds will be impossible to find. But don't despair. You can see all the greats up close—even take their pictures—during the practice rounds preceding the tournament. The bad news is the **Masters Practice Rounds** have become so popular that tickets must now be purchased in advance, $16 to $21 per day. To receive an application form write to Masters Tournament Practice Rounds, P.O. Box 2047, Augusta 30903-2047.

If you'd like to play, the **Jones Creek Course,** an 18-hole public layout at 4101 Hammonds Ferry Road, (706) 860–4228, is considered the "poor man's" Augusta National. Designed by renowned golf architect Rees Jones, it has an excellent practice facility and professional instructors. Rental clubs and carts are available.

Ever wondered how a daily newspaper is put together? *The*

Augusta Chronicle-Herald's free tour has all the answers. The one-hour guided tour—by appointment from 10:00 to 11:00 A.M. Fridays—takes you through the busy newsrooms and feature departments and into the printing plant, where type is set and pages assembled and published on high-speed presses. *The Herald* is located at Broad Street, downtown, (706) 724–0851.

The **Telfair Inn,** 326 Greene Street, (404) 724–3315, is a beautiful example of practical restoration. Seventeen Victorian residences were rejuvenated, redecorated, and refurnished in nineteenth-century fashion, with wood-burning fireplaces and all the modern comforts, and turned into a lovely downtown inn. Rates are $57 to $97 single, $67 to $107 double.

Bass fishermen and those seeking more off-the-beaten-path relaxation should look into a minivacation at ❖ **Mistletoe State Park.** About 35 miles north of Augusta, on 76,000-acre Clarks Hill Reservoir, this very tranquil park reputedly commands some of America's finest bass fishing waters. You may also swim and boat in the lake, hike 5 miles of woodland trails, and ride rental bikes around the 1,920 acres. Two-bedroom furnished cottages and camping sites with water, electricity, showers, and rest rooms are available. There is a $2.00 per visit parking fee. Contact Park Superintendent, Appling 30502, (706) 541–0321. For camping and cottage reservations call (800) 864–PARK.

❖ **Elijah Clark State Park,** north of Mistletoe, is another wooded retreat on the western shores of Clarks Hill Lake. Twenty furnished cottages and 165 tent and trailor sites are a few steps from the water. You'll also find marinas, docks, boat ramps, a swimming beach, nature trails, and plenty of picnic areas. The park was named for Revolutionary War hero Elijah Clark. A Colonial museum displays relics from the period. The park is on Highway 378, 7 miles east of Lincolnton. Phone (706) 359–3458 for information. For reservations call (800) 864–PARK.

Burke County, between Augusta and Savannah, hails itself as "The Bird Dog Capital of the World." You can test its veracity with an organized bird and game hunt at ❖ **Boll Weevil Plantation,** Route 2, Box 356A, Waynesboro 30830, (706) 554–6227. You can stay overnight at **Georgia's Guest Bed & Breakfast,** 640 East Seventh Street, Waynesboro 30830, (706) 554–4863.

COASTAL GEORGIA

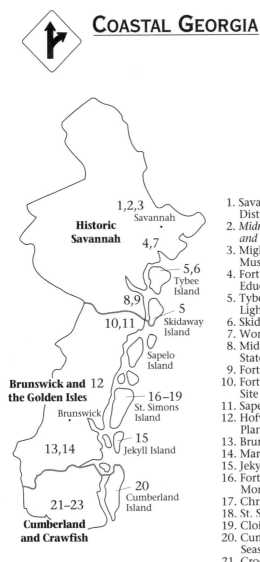

Historic Savannah

1,2,3
Savannah

4,7

5,6
Tybee Island

8,9

5
Skidaway Island

10,11

Sapelo Island

Brunswick and the Golden Isles 12

Brunswick

16–19
St. Simons Island

13,14

15
Jekyll Island

20
Cumberland Island

21–23

Cumberland and Crawfish

1. Savannah National Historic District
2. *Midnight in the Garden of Good and Evil* tours
3. Mighty Eighth Heritage Museum
4. Fort Jackson/Oatland Island Education Center
5. Tybee Island Museum and Lighthouse
6. Skidaway Island State Park
7. Wormsloe State Historic Site
8. Midway Church/Fort Morris State Historic Site
9. Fort Stewart Military Museum
10. Fort King George State Historic Site
11. Sapelo Island Tours
12. Hofwyl-Broadfield Rice Plantation
13. Brunswick
14. Mary Miller Doll Museum
15. Jekyll Island Historic District
16. Fort Frederica National Monument
17. Christ Church
18. St. Simons Lighthouse
19. Cloister Hotel
20. Cumberland Island National Seashore
21. Crooked River State Park
22. Woodbine Crawfish Festival
23. Marshlands Plantation Crawfish Farm

COASTAL GEORGIA
HISTORIC SAVANNAH

Founded in 1733 as the seat of England's Georgia Crown Colony, Savannah is one of America's truly special cities. The founding father, General James Edward Oglethorpe, planned the city on a precise grid of broad, straight thoroughfares intersecting public squares at regular intervals. Initially conceived as mustering places for militia, the squares eventually became public gardens, embellished with fountains, trees, flowers, and monuments to Revolutionary heroes. In the prosperous years before the Civil War, wealthy cotton brokers and shipbuilders flanked the squares with stately residences in English Regency, Federal, Georgian, Neo-Gothic, and other styles.

A post–Civil War collapse of the cotton market inadvertently saved much of this noble architecture from destruction. Since the mid-1950s, an ongoing campaign has restored nearly 2,000 historic residences, churches, and public buildings in the 2.2-square-mile ◆ **Savannah National Historic District,** the largest in the nation. Many visitors from all over the world will discover Savannah in 1996, when the city hosts the summer Olympic Games's yachting events.

One of the simple pleasures of visiting Savannah is sitting in the squares and leisurely admiring the rich ornamental details of the monuments and eighteenth- and nineteenth-century buildings. No matter how many times you've been here, no matter how many times you've looked, you'll always see something that previously eluded your gaze. This intriguing factor makes even the most beaten track into an off-the-beaten-path adventure.

With its compact dimensions and so much to see, Savannah is a walker's delight, especially in spring when millions of azaleas, dogwoods, and other flowering plants turn the whole city into a pastel-shaded movie set. You can also rent bikes or ride in a horse-drawn carriage. Orient yourself to the city by stopping first at the Savannah Visitors Center, in the redbrick, 1860s Central of Georgia Railroad Depot, at 301 Martin Luther King Boulevard, downtown, (912) 944–0456 and (800) 444–2427. Watch an orientation slide show ($1.00 adults, 50 cents children) and pick up brochures, maps, and information about points of interest.

Numerous guided tours in air-conditioned vans leave from the visitors center. If you read John Berendt's best-selling nonfiction book, ◆ *Midnight in the Garden of Good and Evil,* about a scandalous 1980s murder case, you can see many of the scenes and even meet some of the real-life characters on a **Walk the Book Tour** with Tours by BJ, (912) 233–2335. You also can see some of the places where Oscar-winning *Forrest Gump* was filmed. Forrest's bus stop bench—a movie prop removed after the film—was in Chippewa Square.

A city this old naturally (or supernaturally, if you will) has scads of ghosts and rumors of ghosts. You can hear all about them, and get a good case of chill bumps, by going on Jack Richards's **Ghost Talk, Ghost Walk Tours,** (912) 233–3896.

If you're traveling with kids who don't dig Savannah's ancient history, take them on a **Savannah Safari.** With a $5.00 booklet available at Savannah bookstores, this fun "safari" leads you on a search of birds and animals cunningly camouflaged on fountains, gates, houses, churches, door knockers, and downspouts. To make it sporting, each of the fifty-three safari stops has a little rhyme explorers fill in. If you can't find the book or want a guided tour, call (912) 353–9999.

If you are on your own, one of the best places to start is the riverfront. On Bay Street, standing on bluffs above the Savannah River, a row of redbrick buildings know as **Factors Walk** was the hub of Savannah's pre–Civil War cotton economy. The cotton itself was stored in brick warehouses below the offices as it awaited shipment to mills in England and New England. As a major element of the city's rejuvenation, the old brick warehouses have been remodeled as seafood restaurants, taverns, shops, and art galleries and flanked by a broad esplanade called **Riverfront Plaza,** also known as River Street. Benches are excellent places to sit and watch the colossal cargo ships heading for the docks and industries up the Savannah River or to the open Atlantic, 20 miles downriver.

The **Ships of the Sea Museum,** 503 River Street/Riverfront Plaza, (912) 232–1511, is a natural complement to the city's maritime heritage. Three floors shine with ornamental figureheads, scrimshaw artistry, a chandler's shop, ships-in-bottles, sailing ship models, and other artifacts. It's open daily 10:00 A.M. to 5:00 P.M. Adults are $3.00; ages 7 to 12, $1.50.

The museum's top floor is on Bay Street, a convenient starting point for walking tours of the downtown squares and important landmarks. The most popular walking route takes you from the front of Savannah's ornate **City Hall**—the dome was recently regilded—south on Bull Street to **Forsyth Park.** Along the way, you'll cross Johnson, Wright, Chippewa, Madison, and Monterey Squares. Each has a monument to a bygone hero and landmarks that played important parts in the city's history.

Revolutionary War hero General Nathanael Greene is buried beneath the granite shaft in **Johnson Square. Wright Square** honors the founder of the Central of Georgia Railroad.

At Bull Street and Oglethorpe Avenue, Girl Scouts and students of American history should pause at the **Juliette Gordon Low Girl Scout National Center** (912–233–4501). Built in the early nineteenth century by noted English architect William Jay, the dignified English Regency mansion was the 1860 birthplace of "Daisy" Low, founder of the Girl Scouts of America. Daisy's paintings and sculpture, personal effects, and GSA mementos are displayed in the high-ceilinged rooms. It's open Monday through Saturday 10:00 A.M. to 4:00 P.M. and Sunday 12:30 to 4:30 P.M.; closed Wednesday. Adults are $4.00, students, $3.00, under age 6, no charge.

A bronze statue of General Oglethorpe, by Daniel Chester French, highlights **Chippewa Square.** The centerpiece in **Madison Square** honors Sergeant William Jasper, killed in the Revolutionary War battle for the city in 1779. From the **Green-Meldrim House** General William T. Sherman telegraphed President Lincoln a Christmas gift of the city, which had peacefully surrendered on December 14, 1864. It's now the parish house for St. John's Episcopal Church.

The marble column in **Monterey Square** honors Casimir Pulaski, a Polish count who died in the 1779 siege. **Congregation Mickve Israel** (912–233–1547), on the east side of Monterey Square, traces its heritage back to July 11, 1733, only five months after General Oglethorpe established the colony. Some descendants of the original Jewish settlers still worship at the handsome Gothic synagogue, completed in 1878. If you come to the side door Monday through Friday between 10:00 A.M. and noon, a member of the congregation will show you the sanctuary, tell the history of the congregation, and let you browse through a small museum with a deerskin Torah, documents, and ceremonial pieces that date back to the original settlers.

East and west of Bull Street, Whitefield, Lafayette, and Troup Squares are surrounded by restored residences in a variety of architectural styles. The **King-Tisdell Cottage** at 514 East Huntingdon Street (912–234–8000) is headquarters for **Negro Heritage Trail Tours,** which include landmarks of the city's Black history, going back to the arrival of the first slaves. Built in 1896, the cottage is a museum of coastal Georgia Black history and noteworthy for its Victorian furnishings and "gingerbread" ornamentation. Hours are Monday through Friday 10:00 A.M. to 4:30 P.M. and weekends 1:00 to 4:00 P.M. Admission for adults is $1.75; children, 75 cents.

The **Davenport House** on Columbia Square played a vital role in Savannah's restoration movement. Built between 1815 and 1820 and considered one of America's most perfect Georgian mansions, the house was threatened in the 1950s with demolition to make room for a funeral home parking lot. The Historic Savannah Foundation saved the Davenport and has since led the effort to save hundreds of other historic structures. Now a museum, the restored Davenport (912–236–8097) gleams with Chippendale and Sheraton furnishings, woodwork, and plaster crown moldings. Visitors are welcome Monday to Saturday 10:00 A.M. to 4:30 P.M. and Sunday 1:30 to 4:30 P.M. Admission fees are adults $4.00, children $3.00. (Incidentally, the funeral home has come back to life as a European-style small hotel.)

The Marquis de Lafayette slept at the **Owens-Thomas House** (912–233–9743) on nearby Oglethorpe Square during an 1825 farewell tour of the young nation he'd helped so significantly to establish. Guided tours point out the side balcony from which he addressed the populace, his bedroom, and numerous priceless antiques and artworks. Located at 124 Abercorn Street, it's open Tuesday through Saturday 10:00 A.M. to 5:00 P.M.; Sunday and Monday 2:00 to 5:00 P.M. Admission is charged: adults $5.00, students $3.00, ages 6 to 12, $2.00, under age 6, no charge.

On Telfair Square, the **Telfair Mansion and Museum,** 121 Barnard Street (912–232–1177), is a splendid English Regency masterpiece in its own right. On display are decorative pieces, English and American art and furnishings. It's open Tuesday through Saturday 10:00 A.M. to 5:00 P.M. and Sunday 2:00 to 5:00 P.M. Adults are $2.00; students and senior citizens, $1.00; free for all on Sunday.

The ◆ **Mighty Eighth Heritage Museum**—scheduled to open in spring 1996—will honor the Eighth Air Force, which was formed in Savannah in 1942 and served valiantly throughout

World War II in Europe. The 90,000-square-foot museum, at I–95 and Highway 80, will include historic displays, audiovisuals, a library, and other exhibits portraying the "Mighty Eighth's" heroic accomplishments. Call (800) 421–9428 for information.

Some of Savannah's most interesting dining experiences are linked to its history. Here are a few local favorites:

At the **Boar's Head,** take a table in one of the candlelit, stone-walled dining rooms or on the outdoor patio and watch big cargo ships sail by as you dig into first-class steaks, seafood, pasta, veal, and lamb dishes. One of the city's oldest restaurants, the Boar's Head, River Street at Lincoln, (912) 232–3196, is still among the best.

At **Il Pasticcio,** (912) 231–8888, dine on fresh pastas, grilled vegetables, shrimp risotto, oak-fired pizza, rotisserie chicken, real Italian gelato, fresh baked goods, and sensational *tiramisu* and other worth-the-calorie desserts while you watch the crowds go by the corner of busy Bull and Broughton Streets downtown. A good selection of American and Italian wines is available by the bottle or glass. The restaurant is a cleverly converted art deco women's dress shop with floor-to-ceiling windows. Before or after lunch or dinner, browse owner/artist Floriana Venetico's second-floor art gallery.

For a treat for your "soul," come for weekday lunch at **Nita's Place,** a stellar soul food eatery in the historic district at 140 Abercorn Street, (912) 238–8233. Owner and chef Nita Dixon is one of Savannah's most congenial hosts. Her fried chicken, crab cakes, seafood gumbo, and corn bread are killers.

For a special treat make dinner reservations at **Elizabeth on 37th.** Chef Elizabeth Terry has garnered scores of national culinary awards for her cuisine, which intricately combines fresh local ingredients with classical preparation. Seafood dishes and desserts are especially recommended. It's in a former sugar baron's Victorian mansion at 105 East 37th Street, on the edge of the historic district; phone (912) 236–5547.

Long-time landmark **Clary's,** corner of West Jones and Abercorn Streets, (912) 233–0402, has gotten all dressed up since its appearance in *Midnight in the Garden of Good and Evil.* (Loopy Luther Driggers reputedly plotted to poison Savannah's water supply over daily breakfast at Clary's.) The old drugstore and lunch counter have been replaced by a bright, cheerful cafe splashed with old Savannah photos and murals and serving

1990s-style breakfast and lunch daily. Ballast yourselves for the day with "Hoppel Poppel," a breakfast concoction of scrambled eggs with chunks of kosher salami, potatoes, onions, and green peppers, and served with grits and biscuit or bagel. Lunch is a choice of homemade soups, big sandwiches, salads, and burgers.

For a memorable musical taste of Savannah, spend an evening with pianist and chanteuse **Emma Kelly at Hannah's East,** a cozy jazz room in The Pirates' House restaurant, 20 East Broad Street, (912) 233–2225. Her mentor, Savannah songwriter Johnny Mercer, hailed Emma as "Savannah's Lady of 6,000 Songs"—by now she knows many more than that. She's featured in *Midnight in the Garden of Good and Evil.*

Crystal Beer Parlor, a comfortable old tavern on 301 West Jones Street at Jefferson Street (912–232–1153), has served delicious fried oyster sandwiches, state-of-the-art onion rings, gumbo, hamburgers, and seafood chowder to generations of Savannahians and visitors. Children are welcome. It's inexpensive, open Monday through Saturday, and accepts major credit cards.

Something of a paradox, **Mrs. Wilkes Boardinghouse,** probably Savannah's best-known dining room, is hidden unpretentiously away in the historic district at 107 West Jones Street, (912) 232–5997. You know you're there by the long lines waiting outside. Family-style lunch includes endless portions of fried chicken, fried fish, barbecue, vegetables, corn bread, biscuits, and dessert. Breakfast features eggs, sausage, biscuits, and buttered grits. Very inexpensive breakfast and lunch are available Monday through Friday; no credit cards are accepted.

The **City Market,** a once-neglected row of warehouses on West Congress, West St. Julian, and Barnard Streets, near the riverfront, is alive again. You can browse in more than two dozen artist studios and shops and enjoy casual dining and nighttime entertainment in some of the city's most popular bistros.

Bistro Savannah, 309 West Congress Street, (912) 233–6266, features spicy vindaloo chicken, Louisiana jambalaya, and revolving exhibitions by local artists.

Express Cafe and Bakery, 39 Barnard Street, (912) 233–4683, serves pastries, croissants, gourmet sandwiches, and soups and salads in a handsome black-and-white tiled former drugstore.

Horsedrawn carriage tours of the historic district also begin and end at the City Market.

To experience Savannah's Old World charisma thoroughly, stay overnight in an historic inn or bed and breakfast. More than two dozen are situated in vintage mansions and townhouses, furnished with antiques and artworks. Rates usually include breakfast, afternoon wine or tea, and a late-night liqueur. Some of the most atmospheric include **Ballastone Inn,** 14 East Oglethorpe Avenue, (912) 236–1484; **Bed and Breakfast Inn,** 117 West Gordon Street, (912) 238–0518; **Habersham At York Inn,** Habersham and York Streets, (912) 234–2499; **East Bay Inn,** 225 East Bay Street, (912) 238–1225; **Gastonian Inn,** 220 East Gaston Street, (912) 232–2869; **Magnolia Place Inn,** 503 Whitaker Street, (912) 236–2869; and **Planters Inn,** 29 Abercorn Street, (912) 232–5678.

For reservations at these and other historic inns, call these central services: R.S.V.P. Savannah, (912) 232–7787 or (800) 729–7787; and Savannah Historic Inns and Guest Houses, (912) 233–7666 or (800) 262–4667.

Some of Savannah's most intriguing off-the-beaten-path attractions are away from the downtown historic district on outlying beaches and coastal islands. First head east to Fort Jackson, Fort Pulaski, and the beaches and historic sites on Tybee Island.

♦ **Fort Jackson,** on Highway 80/Islands Expressway 3 miles east of downtown, was constructed along the Savannah River in various stages between 1808 and 1879. All shipping bound for Savannah's port had to pass by the fort's heavy guns. A tidal moat still girds the sturdy brick walls. Artifacts include cannon, small arms, machinery, and tools that are demonstrated at yearly special events. In the summer, cannon firings and military drills are conducted by uniformed soldiers at 1 Fort Jackson Road. The fort (912–232–3945) is open daily 9:00 A.M. to 5:00 P.M. Adults are $2.00; students, military, and senior citizens, $1.50.

♦ **Oatland Island Education Center,** just off the Islands Expressway east of the Wilmington River, is a fascinating nature experience for all ages. Operated by the Savannah-Chatham Public Schools, the center is a focus of nature education programs and special activities. Even on a short visit, you may walk through a nature trail and see an astonishing variety of wildlife. In secured natural habitats you'll observe alligators, wolves, bobcats, bears, panthers, deer, bald eagles, egrets, heron, lizards, and many other creatures. Located at 711 Sandtown Road (912–897–3773), it's open Monday through Friday 8:30 A.M. to

5:00 P.M. and October to May the second Saturday of the month 11:00 A.M. to 5:00 P.M. There is an admission fee: one can of cat or dog food per person.

Fort Pulaski National Monument, off Highway 80, guards the Savannah River entrance from the Atlantic Ocean. The star-shaped fortress took eighteen years to construct—a young West Point engineering graduate named Robert E. Lee lent his exper-tise—but surrendered to Union forces on April 11, 1862, follow-ing a brief but devastating attack by the new cannon rifles. Maintained by the National Park Service, the fort's visitors cen-ter—Cockspur Island, 15 miles east of downtown, (912) 786–5787—has historical exhibits, weapons, and uniforms. Admission from March 1 to Labor Day is $1.00 adults; under 16 and over 62, no charge; maximum for carload, $3.00. The rest of year it's free for all.

There's nothing chic or glamorous about **Tybee Island**—in truth, it's the very antithesis of rich and fashionable Southern resorts such as South Carolina's Hilton Head Island. And therein lies the charm of this comfortable old shoe of a beach and summer home island, 20 miles east of downtown Savannah. Many Savannah families spend the torrid summers in cottages near the beach, where a mild Atlantic surf laps 3 miles of hard-packed sands.

In warm weather, you'll probably want to make a beeline for one of the Tybee beaches. The most popular locale for swimming and sunbathing is the commercial area around Butler Avenue and 16th Street—a funky, old-fashioned–looking place straight from Coney Island, circa 1940. Here you'll find ice-cream and fudge shops, chair and beach umbrella vendors, a fishing pier, small motels and cottages, public rest rooms, and changing rooms and showers.

Throughout the year don't miss the ◆ **Tybee Island Museum and Lighthouse.** Housed inside a Spanish American War coastal artillery battery, the museum is like a trip through an incredible attic. On display are Civil War rifles, flintlock pistols, a pictorial history of the island, old newspapers and magazines, old marriage licenses, a plaster pietà, antique dolls, shrunken heads, ancient armor, homage to Savannah's world-famous song-writer Johnny Mercer, stuffed birds and butterflies, Nazi flags and Japanese samurai swords, an English whiskey still, a World War II exhibit with propaganda leaflets, and a model of the cotton gin

115

that Connecticut Yankee Eli Whitney invented during a 1793 Savannah vacation. You may view the beach from the outdoor observation platform.

You may also climb the spiraling 178 steps to the top of the adjacent lighthouse, which was completed in 1867 and rises 145 feet. After huffing and puffing to the top, you'll be rewarded with scenic views from the observation deck. The museum is open April 1 to September 30 daily 10:00 A.M. to 6:00 P.M. and October 1 to March 31 Monday to Friday 1:00 to 5:00 P.M. and Saturday and Sunday 10:00 A.M. to 5:00 P.M. Adults are $1.00; ages 12 and under are free when accompanied by an adult. Call (912) 786–4077. The lighthouse (912–786–5801) is open April through September 10:00 A.M. to 6:00 P.M. daily except Tuesday; October through March daily except Tuesday 12:00 to 4:00 P.M. Adults are $1.50; ages 6 to 12, 50 cents when accompanied by an adult.

Moderately priced accommodations on the beach include the **Days Inn Tybee Island** (912–786–4576) and the **DeSoto Beach Motel** (912–786–4542).

The **Hunter House Bed and Breakfast,** Butler Avenue at Seventeenth Street, Tybee Island 31328, (912) 786–7515, captures Tybee's laid-back beach ambience. Simply furnished, unfussy rooms range from singles to four-room suites. Some have kitchens, even fireplaces for chilly winter days by the sea, a block away. The upstairs restaurant and bar, with an outside deck, is a popular gathering place for islanders and specializes in coastal seafood, steaks, pastas, and stout drinks. If you lend an ear during afternoon happy hour, you'll pick up on the skinny on just about everything that's happening on the island. Be careful, though. Islanders are so sold on Tybee, they'll have you packing up and moving down before you know it. Hunter House rates are moderate and seasonal.

After an energetic day at the beach, head for **Williams Seafood,** Highway 80 at the Bull River Bridge, (912) 897–2219, for simply prepared fried and broiled seafood at very low prices. It's open for lunch and dinner daily, no credit cards accepted. You may also join swarms of locals and tourists fishing for their sustenance off the bridges.

Savannah restaurateur Linda Davis scored an immediate smash hit when she opened **Goodfriends Galley,** (912) 897–0990, in 1995. Across Highway 80 from Williams Seafood, the Galley's twenty-four seats are on the screened porch of Bull River Marina, overlooking fishing and pleasure boats bobbing at the wooden docks. Eager eaters pack the place every night for an ever-changing selection of stuffed flounder, schnitzel, shrimp scampi, oysters, lamb, veal, fresh fish, and other surprises. Reservations are advised. Lunch and dinner are served Tuesday to Sunday, breakfast Saturday and Sunday.

Spanky's Beachside, 404 Butler Avenue, (912) 786–5520, and **The Crab Shack,** 40-A Estill Hammock Road, (912) 786–9857, are also popular drop-ins for seafood, salads, sandwiches, and cold drinks.

You can rent a beachfront condo, cottage, or beach house through **Tybee Island Rentals,** P.O. Box 1440, Tybee Island 31328, (800) 755–8562 or (912) 786–8805.

If you'd like to try out your fishing skills or take a nature cruise through the islands, check with **Tybee Marina,** 1315 Chatham Avenue, (912) 786–7508, or **Lazaretto Creek Marina,** One Old Highway 80, (912) 786–5848.

Skidaway Island, south of downtown, has its own trove of off-the-beaten-path adventures. ◆ **Skidaway Island State Park,** off Diamond Causeway, (912) 598–2300, is a 490-acre preserve that's relaxed and quiet even in the busiest seasons. The one hundred tent and trailer camping sites ($10 a night) have water and electrical connections, showers, and rest rooms. Amenities include a swimming pool, picnic shelters, nature trails and weekend nature programs, and a playground. There's no beach (or fishing) inside the park, but there are plenty of opportunities for both nearby. There is a $2.00 per visit parking fee.

The **Skidaway Island Marine Extension Center** (912–356–2496), operated by the University of Georgia, includes an excellent small aquarium. The twelve tanks house a colorful array of coastal fish, including moray eels, barracuda, catfish, pigfish, moonfish, pompano, squirrel fish, and porcupine fish. It's open Monday through Friday 9:00 A.M. to 4:00 P.M. and Saturday and Sunday noon to 5:00 P.M. It's on McWhorter Drive, off Diamond Causeway.

At ◆ **Wormsloe State Historic Site,** a picturesque and very photogenic 1½-mile avenue of live oaks leads to the tabby ruins of a colonial estate built by Noble Jones, one of the original contingent of settlers who arrived with General James Edward Oglethorpe in 1733. The visitors center displays artifacts excavated on the estate and an audiovisual show about the founding of the Georgia Crown Colony. You may walk a nature trail to the Jones family gravesite and tabby foundations of their eighteenth-century home. During special times of the year such as Christmas season, Memorial Day, Labor Day, and Georgia Week in February, staff in period dress demonstrate colonial crafts and skills. Located at 7601 Skidaway Road (912–352–2548), it's open Tuesday through Saturday 9:00 A.M. to 5:00 P.M. and Sunday 2:00 to 5:30 P.M.

The nearby **Isle of Hope** is another picturesque place for a drive or walk. Go to the end of LaRoche Avenue and follow Bluff Drive along the Wilmington River. The many lovely homes and a frame Roman Catholic church are set off by towering live oaks and banks of azaleas.

Fort McAllister State Historic Park, 25 miles south of Savannah in Bryan County, is highlighted by the best preserved earthwork fortifications anywhere in the old Confederacy. Built on bluffs above the south bank of the Great Ogeechee River, the earthworks withstood seven Union land and sea assaults before finally capitulating in December 1864. It was the last major obstacle on General William T. Sherman's "March to the Sea" and led to Savannah's peaceful surrender shortly thereafter. The earthworks and heavy guns have been restored to their wartime appearance. The museum and visitors center has Civil War weapons and other artifacts.

Also part of Fort McAllister is a recreation area (912–727–2339) with seventy-five tent and trailer camping sites, with electricity, water, rest rooms and showers, picnic tables and grills, 5 miles of hiking trails, boat ramps, and docks. There is a $2.00 per visit parking fee. To get there follow Highway 144, 10 miles east of I–95 exit 15. Call (800) 864–PARK for reservations.

As you drive along Highway 17 between Savannah and Brunswick, ◆**Midway Church** looms out of the gnarled arms of a live oak grove, looking like a New England meeting-house that's lost its way. In fact, the white clapboard church, with its gabled roof and square belfry, traces its heritage to Massachusetts Puritans, who founded the Midway Society in 1754. The present church dates from 1792. Illustrious parishioners have included two signers of the Declaration of Independence and Theodore Roosevelt's great-grandfather. The fathers of Oliver Wendell Holmes and Samuel F. B. Morse have served as pastor.

Pick up the big iron key at the BP station or the Midway Museum. The unadorned church interior has straightback pews and a slave gallery. Across the highway, the churchyard is the resting place of Midway's founders and Revolutionary War heroes. The adjacent **Midway Museum,** open Tuesday through Saturday 10:00 A.M. to 4:00 P.M. and Sunday 2:00 to 4:00 P.M., (912) 884–5837, has colonial furnishings, documents, and exhibits. Adults are $1.00; ages 12 and under, 50 cents.

You can really forsake the beaten path by taking Highway 38 14 miles east of Midway, to the ◆ **Fort Morris State Historic Site.** The curator at the small museum there will relate the history of this vanished colonial seaport and point out the ruins of Fort Morris, a bulwark against British attack during the American Revolution and the War of 1812. Admission for adults is $2.00; children, $1.00. Phone (912) 884–5999.

West of Midway, via Highway 84, the U.S. Army's ◆ **Fort Stewart Military Museum** (912–767–4891) displays uniforms, weapons, flags, photos, and vehicles from the Civil War through the Persian Gulf War. It is open daily 10:00 A.M. to 6:00 P.M. Stimulated by Fort Stewart's large payroll, nearby Hinesville is full of motels, shopping centers, and restaurants serving everything from fast food and American dishes to German, Chinese, Mexican, and Korean cuisine.

BRUNSWICK AND THE GOLDEN ISLES

This coastal county, between Savannah and Brunswick, was the site of a British fort that predated Georgia's founding as a colony in 1733. Marshy bays and coastal islands are home to national marine and wildlife refuges and picturesque fleets of fishing boats and shrimping trawlers.

Stop first at the Darien Welcome Center (912–437–6684), on Highway 17 at the Darien River bridge for general information and reservations for Sapelo Island tours. The ◆ **Fort King George State Historic Site,** a mile off Highway 71, (912) 437–4770, marks an earthwork and palisaded log fortress built by South Carolinians in 1721 to fend off Spanish advances from Florida. Most of the fort was destroyed by fire in 1726.

A state visitors center and museum has displays, artifacts, and

119

Fort King George

a film of the fort and early Georgia life and is open Tuesday through Saturday 9:00 A.M. to 5:00 P.M. and Sunday 2:00 to 5:30 P.M. Adults are $2.00; ages 6 to 12, $1.00. On the way to the fort site, you may stop and photograph Darien's shrimp fleet and **St. Cyprian's Episcopal Church** (1870), Darien's first Black house of worship.

Open Gates Bed & Breakfast, Vernon Square, Darien 31305, (912) 437–6985, is a gem of a country inn. Every room in the century-old home is like a page from a glossy home-and-garden magazine. Owners Carolyn and Philip Hodges have embellished guest rooms with American and European antiques, family heirlooms and portraits, handmade quilts, and china. The house is comfortably air-conditioned and has a small swimming pool. The Hodges are a wealth of information about off-the-beaten-path places to visit and photograph. Rates of $45 to $55 for a double include an ample continental breakfast.

From Darien, Highway 99 meanders 16.3 miles along the marshes, low country, and fishing villages that make McIntosh County special. At Meridian you'll catch the state-operated ferry to Sapelo Island. Go north another 1.6 miles, look for a sign to Valona, a few docks, and a post office with plenty of opportunities to photograph the shrimping trawlers. (Valona was named for an Albanian fishing port!)

Highway 99 loops back into Highway 17 and I–95 at Eulonia. If you're anywhere around Eulonia at dinnertime, make tracks for **The Buccaneer,** (912) 832–5171, a humble waterside restaurant that turns Low Country seafood into an art form.

At South Newport, north of Eulonia, you can "Rub Elbows With God" at what's purportedly the smallest church in America. **Christ Chapel** seats twelve for services every third Sunday. The stained-glass windows were imported from England.

◆ **Sapelo Island Tours,** conducted by the Georgia Department of Natural Resources, take you through the fascinating ecology of the Sapelo Island National Estuarine Sanctuary. On the thirty-minute ferry trip from Meridian, you'll skirt wavering stands of cord grass marsh and scores of small islets and hammocks. Touring the island on a bus or tram, see the exterior of a mansion built by tobacco baron R. J. Reynolds. Naturalists will show you how to seine a flounder, explain some of the mysteries of the marshes, and point out deer, wild turkeys, and many species of waterfowl that call the island home. You'll have time to walk the beaches and collect shells. The island's facilities are limited to rest rooms, water fountains, and soft drink machines. Bring a snack, if you wish, and don't forget the insect repellent!

Tours are conducted year-round on Wednesday 8:30 A.M. to 12:30 P.M. and Saturday 9:00 A.M. to 1:00 P.M. Friday tours are conducted from June through Labor Day. Extended day tours are offered the last Tuesday of the month from March through October from 8:30 A.M. to 2:30 P.M. Bring a picnic lunch. Required reservations are made through the Darien Welcome Center, Box 1497, Darien 31305, (912) 437–6684. No tickets are sold at the Meridian dock. It costs $10.00 for adults; $6.00 for ages 6 to 18; under age 6, free.

◆ **Hofwyl-Broadfield Rice Plantation,** on U.S. Highway 17, 6 miles south of Darien, is a reminder of the rice culture that once flourished along the Altamaha River. Stop by the state park's visitors center and view the slide presentation, then take a 1-mile walking tour above the overgrown rice fields and to the main house. The plantation was owned by one family from 1806 to 1973, and the simple white frame house, circa 1850, has many original furnishings.

It's open Tuesday through Saturday 9:00 A.M. to 5:00 P.M. and Sunday 2:00 to 5:30 P.M. Adults are $2.00; ages 6 to 18, $1.00; under age 6, no charge. Phone (912) 264–9263.

"The Golden Isles" are a necklace of lush, subtropical barrier islands that serpentine languidly along Georgia's Atlantic coast for more than 120 miles. Several of the principal islands accessible to visitors are part of Glynn County. Even the most highly developed islands—St. Simons and Jekyll—are low-key, laid-back, and lightly commercialized when compared with other resort islands along the Eastern Seaboard. And with their long stretches of beaches, marshes, inlets, rivers, and live oak forests, it's very easy to get off the beaten path and commune in solitude with untrampled nature.

◆ **Brunswick,** the Glynn County seat and a center of Georgia's shrimping and oystering industries, is a gateway to Jekyll, St. Simons, Sea, and Little St. Simons islands. Like Savannah, Brunswick was laid out in the eighteenth century on a precise grid, with public squares at regular intervals. Included on the National Register of Historic Places since 1978, many homes and public buildings on Union, Reynolds, Egmont, Prince, London, Dartmouth, and other British-sounding streets date back to the early and mid-nineteenth century. Gingerbread and wrought-iron–trimmed showplaces in Queen Anne, Gothic, Italianate, mansard, and Jacobean style are enhanced by towering live oaks, banks of azaleas, and dogwoods and camellias.

Pick up maps and information at the Brunswick–Golden Isles Visitors Center at Highway 17 and the F. J. Torras/St. Simons Island Causeway. It's open daily except holidays 9:00 A.M. to 5:00 P.M., (912) 264–5337. In Brunswick the turreted Queen Anne–style **City Hall** dates back to 1883. The **Glynn County Courthouse,** nearby at Reynolds and G Streets, is one of the Southeast's most beautiful. The classical building, topped by a cupola, sits in the midst of a minibotanical garden of moss-draped live oaks, Chinese pistachio, magnolia, and swamp holly trees and flowering shrubbery.

Young ladies in your entourage will enjoy the ◆**Mary Miller Doll Museum,** 1523 Glynn Avenue (912–267–7569). The museum's more than 4,000 dolls include pre–Civil War china heads, bisques, early vinyls, carved woodens, foreign dolls, antique travel cases, and hundreds of dresses and accessories. Open Monday through Saturday 11:00 A.M. to 5:00 P.M. Adults are $2.00; ages 5 to 15, $1.50, under age 5, no charge.

If you'd like to try your hand at deep sea fishing or just get out on the open sea for a spell of quiet relaxation, you'll find numerous boats available for charter around the Brunswick docks at the end of Gloucester Street. Check with the Brunswick–Golden Isles Tourist and Convention Bureau, 4 Glynn Avenue, Brunswick 31520, (912) 265–0620, for specials.

The Royal Cafe, 1618 Newcastle Street, (912) 262–1402, is downtown Brunswick's classiest restaurant. Trendy salmon-shaded walls and Renoir reproductions set the stage for chef/owner A. B. Bakhshizad's menu, which varies from basic burgers to grouper burgers, soft-shell crab, barbecued lamb, pastas, and seafood bisques and other daily soup surprises. Lunch is served weekdays, dinner Friday and Saturday.

Beautifully restored Victorian mansions in the downtown historic district welcome bed-and-breakfast guests. **Brunswick Manor,** built in 1886 as the home of a former Union Army officer, is decorated with Victorian antiques and furnishings. Four suites in the redbrick Victorian Romanesque mansion, now owned by Connecticut transplants Claudia and Harry Tzucanow, have queen-size beds and private baths. Two have kitchens and

123

breakfast nooks. A separate three-bedroom cottage sleeps eight. You can sail around the Golden Isles on the Tzucanows' 51-foot ketch or 39-foot cruiser. Full breakfast is included in rates of $55–$100. Brunswick Manor is located at 825 Egmont Street, Brunswick 31525, (912) 265–6889.

Rose Manor, at 1108 Richmond Street, Brunswick 31525, (912) 267–6369, is also filled with Victorian furnishings and antiques and all the contemporary comforts. Innkeeper Rachel Rose sends off her guests with an enormous Southern breakfast, which is included in the $50–$120 rates.

You can also buy shrimp, oysters, blue crabs, flounder, and other fish fresh off the boats and prepare them yourself.

A causeway ($2.00 per car) connects Brunswick with **Jekyll Island.** Stop first at the Jekyll Island Welcome Center, at the island end of the causeway, (912) 635–3636; toll-free (800) 841–6586. It's open daily 9:00 A.M. to 5:00 P.M.

Between 1886 and 1942, Jekyll was the winter home of some of America's richest and most illustrious families. From the Gilded Age until the beginning of World War II, Astors, Pulitzers, Vanderbilts, Morgans, Rockefellers, Cranes, Goodyears, and other aristocrats lived in secluded luxury on this remote Georgia island. Shortly after Pearl Harbor, they boarded up their elegant "cottages" and left the island for the last time. After the war, the state of Georgia paid $675,000 for the island and turned it into a state park.

One side of the island is skirted by nearly 10 miles of hard-packed Atlantic beaches, washed by a mild surf that's perfect for small children and waders. Free showers, rest rooms, and changing rooms are at regular intervals along the beachfront. Even on the busiest holiday weekends, there's plenty of room to get away from everybody else. The other side is flanked by the Intracoastal Waterway and scenic salt marshes. Deer, raccoon, armadillo, and wild turkey roam in live oak, magnolia, and pine forests.

Tours of the ✦ **Jekyll Island Historic District** begin at the Museum Orientation Center. View a free audiovisual presentation, and then board a motorized tram for a ninety-minute tour that takes you through William Rockefeller's Cape Cod–style **Indian Mound Cottage,** the restored and furnished **Dubignon farmhouse,** and sculpture and furniture exhibits in the restored **Mistletoe Cottage.** Tours are daily 10:00 A.M. to 3:00 P.M. Adults are $8.00; ages 6 to 18, $6.00; under age 6, no charge. Phone (912) 635–4036.

In addition to the beach, Jekyll's recreational outlets include sixty-three holes of golf, indoor and outdoor tennis, rental bikes, fishing, a water slide and wave pool park, picnic grounds, and hiking.

Lodgings include campgrounds with water and electrical hookups, nine hotels widely spaced along the beachfront, and the glamorous and deluxe Jekyll Club Hotel on the Intracoastal Waterway. In the island's "Golden Age," the Jekyll Club was the millionaires' dining area, social center, and guest lodgings. A $20-million restoration has brought it splendidly back to life. Even if you're not staying there, walk through the lobbies and public rooms and admire the stained glass, plaster molding, and other rich architectural details. Contact the hotel at 371 Riverview Drive, Jekyll Island 31527; toll-free (800) 333–3333. It's very expensive.

St. Simons Island, also reached by causeway from Brunswick, is the most popular of the "Golden Isles," but hotels, shopping, and other tourist amenities haven't dimmed the natural splendor of salt marshes, beaches, and stately live oaks veiled in Spanish moss. On the island you may swim and sunbathe on long strands of beaches—all Georgia beaches are public domain—fish, ride horseback, and enjoy historic sites dating back to the early eighteenth century.

❖ **Fort Frederica National Monument,** at the island's northern end, includes remnants of a fortress built by the British in the early 1730s as a guardian against Spanish attack from Florida. Leading up to the fort are the foundations of homes and shops occupied by 1,500 soldiers and civilians. The fort was never tested. The Spanish did come, in 1742, and their defeat at the nearby Battle of Bloody Marsh left England firmly in control of Georgia's coast. Stop first at the National Park Service Visitors Center (912–638–3639) for a film and historical displays. It's open daily 9:00 A.M. to 5:00 P.M. Adults are $1.00; children, 16 and under, free.

❖ **Christ Church,** a Gothic wooden structure on the road to Fort Frederica, is the island's most beloved landmark. The site of services conducted by John and Charles Wesley for Frederica's garrison, the original church was built in 1820. Desecrated by

125

Jekyll Island Club House

Union soldiers, it was rebuilt in 1884 by the Reverend Anson Phelps Dodge, whose life was chronicled by St. Simons resident Eugenia Price in her novel *Beloved Invader*. The church is framed by an arbor of live oaks, dogwoods, and azaleas, and the interior is illuminated by stained-glass windows. It's open daily; donations are welcome. Episcopal services are conducted on Sunday.

At the south end of the island, near the causeway entrance, ❖ **St. Simons Lighthouse** has been a landmark since 1872. The **Museum of Coastal History** in the lightkeeper's cottage displays collections of colonial furniture, shipbuilding tools, and changing exhibitions of coastal art. It's open Tuesday to Sunday 10:00 A.M. to 5:00 P.M. Adults are $3.00; ages 6 to 12, $1.00.

Neptune Park, around the lighthouse, has seaside picnic tables, a playground, and steps down to the beach. You can surf fish from the beach or take a cooler and lawn chair onto the **Municipal Pier** and angle for flounder and whiting and even pull up a startled hammerhead shark or barracuda on occasion. No license is required for saltwater fishing..

Massingale Beach, on Ocean Boulevard, between the King & Prince Hotel and the U.S. Coast Guard Station, has free showers, rest rooms, picnic tables, and a snack bar just off the beach. Don't be disappointed because the Atlantic isn't brilliant turquoise and emerald. Rivers emptying into the ocean give it a silt rather than a sand bottom and turn the waters grayish green.

If you're on a budget, make reservations at **Queen's Court,** an old-fashioned but clean and comfortable motel with some kitchenette rooms near the lighthouse and Neptune Park at 437 Kings Way, St. Simons Island 31522, (912) 638–8459.

Epworth-by-the-Sea, a Methodist conference center, spiritual retreat, and vacation center has 600 modern motel rooms, an inexpensive cafeteria, tennis, fishing, and swimming at moderate rates. You don't have to be Methodist, but alcohol, unmarried couples, and rowdy behavior aren't tolerated. Write to the center at Box 407, St. Simons Island 31522, or call (912) 638–8688.

Although many resort island restaurants come and go like the tides, **Blanche's Courtyard,** 440 Ocean Boulevard, (912) 638–3030, has withstood vacationers' fickle tastes for more than twenty years. In historic St. Simons Village, near the Lighthouse and Municipal Pier, Blanche's continuing popularity stems from its charming, tropical ambience—a 300-year-old oak tree is the centerpiece—and the steady high quality of its fish, seafood, and steaks. Seafood chowders and flounder, shrimp and oysters—prepared a variety of ways—are big favorites. Steaks are also first-rate. Cocktails and wines are available. After dinner, sit back and sing along with the "Good Old Boys" ragtime band, which has delighted Blanche's patrons almost since day one.

Also in The Village, **The Fourth of May Cafe & Deli**'s daily Potluck Specials—a meat or seafood entree with two fresh vegetables for $5.95—is one of the island's tastiest bargains. They also make whopping big deli sandwiches, soups, and salads and belt-loosening desserts. Lunch and dinner are served daily. The Fourth of May is located at 321 Mallery Street, (912) 638–5444.

Up the way at 407 Mallery Street, **J. Mac's Island Restaurant & Jazz Bar,** (912) 634–0403, is a cool, classy place for rack of lamb, soft-shell crab, veal and steaks, cocktails and wine, and entertainment by top-notch jazz exponents.

Mullet Bay, in The Village at 512 Ocean Boulevard, (912) 634–9977, has the casual, breezy ambience of Key West and the Caribbean.

Saint Simons Inn by the Lighthouse, P.O. Box 20225, St. Simons Island 31522, (912) 638–1101, has thirty-four modern, attractively furnished guest rooms and a pool a short walk from The Village's restaurants and shops. The $85 rate for a double includes continental breakfast.

The world is truly not much with us at **Little St. Simons Island.** By the time we've made the twenty-minute launch crossing from "big" St. Simons, the world's problems have vanished in the sunlight of another glorious coastal morning. A fortunate set of circumstances has left the island—6 miles long by 2 to 3 miles wide—very nearly as nature created it.

Through the 1800s the 10,000 acres were the domain of one rice planter and his descendants. In 1903 a pencil company purchased the island, but when the red cedars proved too wind-twisted for writing instruments, it became an off-the-beaten-path retreat, now open to the public.

Guests stay in rustically comfortable lodges that accommodate up to twenty-four. They dine at communal tables and spend their days exploring 6 miles of wild beaches, crabbing and fishing, and taking nature walks into forests inhabited by deer, raccoon, armadillo, pelicans, red-tail hawks, great blue heron, egret, and more than 200 other species, and alongside marshes and rivers where gators cruise like ironclad vessels.

Full American Plan rates of $300 to $400 a couple a night include all meals, fishing, beach and pool swimming, horseback riding, and transportation from St. Simons Island. Contact Little St. Simons Island, P.O. Box 1078, St. Simons Island 31522, (912) 638-7472.

Sea Island, connected to St. Simons Island by a small bridge, is the home of the renowned ◆ **Cloister Hotel,** one of America's legendary resorts. Even if you're not a guest of this lovely hotel, you may admire the beautifully landscaped grounds and drive by the stately homes lining Sea Island Drive. Nonguests may also play the Cloister's **Sea Island Golf Course** and tennis courts and have lunch or dinner in the dining room. Contact Sea Island 31561, (912) 638-3611. It's very expensive.

Dinner at **The Cloister's Main Dining Room** is from another era—dressy and formal, courtly and unhurried. Gents wear jacket and tie, and ladies dress pretty close to the "nines." Wednesday and Saturday nights are optional black tie. The menu ranges from traditional resort hotel fare—prime rib, filet mignon, stuffed flounder—to more contemporary pasta, seafood, lamb, and chicken dishes. Service is extremely gracious. Breakfast, a staggering buffet spread, and lunch are more casual, but the dress code calls for tasteful sportswear, no shorts, please. Very expensive.

The Cloister also manages the **St. Simons Island Club,** (912) 638-5132, a Low-Country plantation-style dining room open to the public on neighboring St. Simons Island. Among the most called-for dinner entrees are Dover sole, flounder, steaks, shrimp and oyster dishes, innovative pasta, chicken, and veal. Everybody wants to get back to the golf course, so lunch is a more straightforward selection of salads, soups, and sandwiches. The Club also has a popular Sunday brunch.

The **Sea Island Golf Club's Dining Room,** (912) 638-5154, on the golf course at historic Retreat Plantation, is a more casual venue for lunchtime sandwiches, salads, and soups and nightly steaks, chicken, seafood, and prime rib. Weekend buffet dinners are great for families and those who have a hard time making up their minds. It's closed Tuesday.

CUMBERLAND AND CRAWFISH

Southernmost of Georgia's Atlantic coastal counties, Camden is the jumping-off place for the Cumberland Island National Seashore. It's also home for U.S. Navy's Kings Bay Trident Submarine base.

Stretching 18 miles long, by 1 to 2 miles wide, Cumberland is by far the largest of Georgia's barrier islands, and of those open to the public, the most primeval. Like a savory dish, blended of many exotic ingredients, ◆ **Cumberland Island National Seashore** is an intricate web of nature's rarest, most wondrous gifts. Preserved as a National Seashore since 1972 and maintained by the National Park Service, it holds an astonishing treasure of marshes and dunes, pristine beaches, live oak forests, lakes, ponds, estuaries, and inlets.

"Natives" include great blue heron, wood storks, egrets, and dozens of other bird species, many of them rarely seen beyond these shores; giant sea turtles, which plod over the beaches to renew their race; fiddler, hermit and ghost crabs; shrimp, oysters, and flounder; deer, armadillo, mink, wild horses, and wild boar; and playful otters and cruising gators.

Mankind's 4,000-year habitation began with ancient Guale Indians, followed by sixteenth-century Spanish missionaries, eighteenth-century British troops, and pre–Civil War rice, indigo, and cotton planters. Thomas Carnegie, of the Pittsburgh Carnegies, bought the entire island in the 1880s. His family's splendid estates were mostly abandoned when the "Gilded Age" gave way to the "Roaring Twenties," and high society discovered more fashionable wintering destinations. With only a few intrusions, the island has passed into public trust largely as it was created.

Unless you own your own boat, the only way to enjoy Cumberland's glories is via a forty-five-minute ride on *The Cumberland Queen* from St. Marys. With a capacity of 150, the ferry departs daily from mid-May through Labor Day at 9:00 A.M., arriving Cumberland at 9:45 A.M.; and 11:45 A.M., arriving Cumberland at 12:30 P.M. It departs Cumberland at 10:15 A.M., arriving at St. Marys at 11:00 A.M.; and 4:45 P.M., arriving St. Marys at 5:30 P.M. The rest of the year it operates at the same times daily except Tuesday and Wednesday. Including taxes, fares are $10.07 adults, $5.99 ages 12 and under, $7.95 ages 65 and over. From May through September an additional ferry leaves the island at 2:45 P.M. and arrives at St. Marys at 3:30 P.M.

Reservations for the ferries may be made up to eleven months in advance by contacting Cumberland Island National Seashore, P.O. Box 806, St. Marys 31558, (912) 882–4335. Bear in mind that sailing times are exact. If you miss the last ferry from the island, you'll have to hire a boat from St. Marys or Fernandina Beach, Florida.

Campers have a choice of developed and primitive campgrounds. Sea Camp, a five-minute walk from the ferry dock, has bathrooms and hot showers; primitive campsites, a 3½- to 10-mile hike from the dock, have trench latrines and cold water spigots.

If you're a day-tripper, you can hike several nature trails, swim and sun, and view the remains of the Carnegie estates. Park Service rangers lead history and nature walks. There's nothing at all for sale on the island, so remember to bring food, cold drinks, insect repellent, and sunscreen.

The island's only hotel-type lodgings are at the **Greyfield Inn,** a Carnegie family home. Guests sleep in four-poster beds, bathe in claw-footed tubs, and relax amid family portraits and mementos. The unique experience costs $245-$350 a couple per night. All meals, transportation from Fernadina Beach, Florida, and walks with naturalists are included. Contact Drawer B, Fernandina Beach, Florida 32034, (904) 261–6408.

The **Riverview Hotel,** across from the Park Service docks in St. Marys, has comfortable, air-conditioned rooms for $50 a double, including tax and continental breakfast. The hotel's **Seagle's Restaurant**—105 Osborne Street, St. Marys 31558, (912) 882–3242—serves breakfast, local seafood, steaks, beer, and cocktails at moderate prices.

◆ **Crooked River State Park,** outside St. Marys, has a swimming pool, fishing, playgrounds, campsites, and cottages. There is a $2.00 per visit parking fee. Contact 3092 Spur 40, St. Marys 31558. For camping and cottage reservations call (800) 864–PARK.

Goodbread House, a bed-and-breakfast in an 1870s Victorian home at 209 Osborne Street, St. Mary's 31558, (912) 882–7490, is another attractive overnight stop for Cumberland Island explorers. Innkeepers Betty and George Krauss have four guest rooms, each with private bath, and serve a full breakfast in the $65 double rate and $50 single rate. Children are welcome, and pets can stay in the fenced yard.

The ◆ **Woodbine Crawfish Festival** takes over the tiny

Camden County seat the last weekend of April. The chance to see beauty queens, bands, parades, and arts and crafts and put away mountains of delicious crustaceans—fried, gumbo'd, etouf-fée'd, jambalaya'd and boiled in Cajun herbs—lures crowds from all over the Georgia coast, and even down into Florida. Phone (912) 576–3211 for information. Many of the crawfish are raised at ❖**Marshlands Plantation Crawfish Farm,** (912) 576–5778, on the edge of Woodbine. From April to June, you can stop by and carry home a sackful. It's one of only a handful of crawfish farms east of the "mud bugs" home grounds in south-ern Louisiana's Cajun country.

NORTHEAST GEORGIA

9–12   2
14   3   4–8
13 15
20 19   17
21 18
22
1 23   16 30
28
Blue Ridge Mountains
Wineries and
Big Lakes 29
27
24–26   34,35
33

Bulldog Country

31,32
36
38
37

1. Appalachian Trail
2. Chattooga River Rafting
3. Lake Rabun Hotel/Rabun Beach Recreation Area
4. Tallulah Gorge Park and Terrora Park and Campground
5. Penny's Garden
6. Foxfire Museum
7. Black Rock Mountain State Park
8. Moccasin Creek State Park
9. Georgia Mountain Fair
10. "The Reach of Song"
11. Chattahoochee National Forest
12. Brasstown Valley Crowne Plaza Resort
13. Russell-Brasstown Scenic Byway
14. Vogel State Park
15. Lake Winfield Scott Recreation Area
16. Habersham Vineyards
17. Mark of the Potter
18. Babyland General Hospital
19. Old Sautee Store/Stovall Covered Bridge
20. "Alpine Helen"
21. Unicoi State Park/Anna Ruby Falls
22. Dahlonega Courthouse Gold Museum
23. Amicalola Falls State Park
24. Lake Lanier Islands
25. Georgia Mountains Museum
26. Elachee Nature Science Center
27. Hart State Park
28. Tugaloo State Park
29. Victoria Bryant State Park
30. Travelers Rest/Toccoa Falls
31. Chateau Elan Winery
32. Fort Yargo State Park
33. Crawford W. Long Museum
34. Elberton Granite Museum/Georgia Guidestones
35. Bobby Brown State Park/Richard B. Russell State Park
36. University of Georgia
37. Oconee County Welcome Center
38. Watson Mill Bridge State Park

Northeast Georgia

Depending on which direction you've set your hiking boots, the 2,015-mile ✦ **Appalachian Trail** either begins or ends with 79 miles of northeast Georgia mountainland. Many AT veterans acclaim the Georgia section as the most beautiful in all the fourteen states between here and Mount Katahdin, Maine.

The AT's southern terminus is atop 3,782-foot **Springer Mountain,** in Dawson County, 75 miles northeast of Atlanta. An 8-mile approach trail begins at Amicalola Falls State Park. There hikers may camp out, get their gear together, and have their packs weighed by park rangers.

From Springer Mountain the AT's Section I is a 22.3-mile easy-to-strenuous hike to Highway 60 at Woody Gap. Section II, 10.7 miles from Woody Gap to Neels Gap, has just one long uphill stretch and is popular with one-day and weekend hikers. At Neels Gap, the trail crosses Highway 19/129 and goes "indoors" as it passes through a covered breezeway of the **Mountain Crossing/Walasi-Yi Center.** At this stone and log legacy of the 1930s Civilian Conservation Corps (CCC), hikers can get trail information and replenish supplies of dehydrated foods and camping gear. Motorists stop by for mountain handicrafts and short hikes on the trail. Phone (706) 745–6095. From Walasi-Yi, Section III is a moderately difficult 5.7 miles to Tesnatee Gap on the Richard Russell Scenic Highway (Highway 348). Sections IV–VI carry the trail upward and onward. At Bly Gap, near the Rabun County/ Towns County border, you bid adieu to Georgia and cross into the North Carolina Great Smokies. Mount Katahdin, here we come!

Blue Ridge Mountains

In Georgia's far northeast corner, up against the North Carolina and South Carolina borders, Rabun County is the heart of the state's dramatically rugged Blue Ridge Mountain country. About 80 percent of the county is included in national forests and state parks. Outdoor adventures range from tranquil trout fishing in mountain streams, canoeing, swimming, off-the-beaten-path hiking, and browsing for handmade crafts at country stores to the ultimate heart-pounding adventure: ✦ **Chattooga River Rafting.**

Until the early 1970s, when Jon Voight, Burt Reynolds, and the rest of the *Deliverance* movie crew let the world in on the secret, the Chattooga River was the remote domain of mountain folk along the Georgia–South Carolina border. Nowadays daredevils come from early spring through late fall to test their courage against the river's steep sluices, whirlpools, and roller-coaster rapids. To see that they accomplish their missions safely, the U.S. Forest Service licenses professional outfitters to conduct the trips, which are made in sturdy six-person rubber rafts and are led by guides who know every rock and rill along this tempestuous waterway.

Outfitters offer a variety of Chattooga experiences. Beginners usually test their wings on Section III, a seven-hour, 6-mile ride that sweeps them through many of the *Deliverance* landmarks. At lunchtime guides pull a small deli out of their waterproof packs and spread the feast at the foot of a waterfall.

Section III is a mere warm-up for "The Ultimate Challenge," the Chattooga's wild and woolly Section IV. Suggested only for well-seasoned white-water hands in top physical condition, this rip-snorting seven-hour cruise carries you through swiftly moving currents; steep, wooded gorges; up and over, down and around such potential perils as Seven Foot Falls, Corkscrew, and Jawbone. At day's end, the Chattooga finally turns you loose, into the peaceful waters of Tugaloo Lake.

For those who really want to get to the heart of the river, outfitters offer two-day trips, which include overnight camping, a steak dinner, and a bountiful breakfast. Some packages offer the option of lodgings at rustic inns and cabins.

Rates begin at about $24 a person for a three-and-a-half-hour guided trip on the Nantahala River to about $200 a person for a full day, including lunch, on the Chattooga River. Contact Nantahala Outdoor Center, (800) 232–7238; Wildwater Limited, (800) 451–9972; and Southeastern Expeditions, (800) 868–7238.

If the Chattooga sparks memories of *Deliverance,* **Lake Rabun,** near the little town of Tallulah Falls, may remind you of the film *On Golden Pond.* Ringed by the soft green humps of the Blue Ridge Mountains and unpretentious summer cottages, some dating back to the 1920s and 1930s, this small off-the-beaten-path lake is the embodiment of peace and quiet.

Built in 1922, the ◆ **Lake Rabun Hotel** is the perfect complement to the lake. New owners have spruced up the sixteen-room wood and stone lodge, polished the mountain laurel and rhododendron furniture, added baths to some rooms, and put in heat for spring and fall guests. You'll still have to go elsewhere for a television, telephone, or air-conditioning. The only meal is a full continental breakfast, with rolls, doughnuts, cereal, orange juice, fresh fruit, and coffee. What the Lake Rabun does offer are rare tranquility and hospitality that draw guests back year after year. In the evenings you can sit by the flagstone hearth, play parlor games, swap tips on local eateries and "secret" waterfalls, and store up energy for the next day's boating, fishing, and hiking. Doubles, with breakfast, are $65.40. Major credit cards are accepted. Closed December to April. Contact Lake Rabun Hotel, Lakemont 30522, (706) 782–4946.

Fishing boats and canoes may be rented at **Hall's Boat House,** next to the hotel. The **Lake Rabun Road,** which twists and turns about 15 miles between Highway 441 near Tallulah Falls, to Georgia Highway 197, is a very scenic drive. It curves around Lake Rabun and Seed Lake, with many lovely vistas of the water and woodlands. Ask the proprietors of the Lake Rabun Hotel for directions to **High Branch Falls,** also known as Minnehaha Falls. It's a little tricky to find but well worth the search. During the summer ◆ **Rabun Beach Recreation Area,** a state-run facility, is a relaxing place to swim and have a picnic.

Old Highway 441, a curvy two-lane road running north and south between the Lake Rabun crossroads of Lakemont and the Rabun County seat of Clayton, is another picturesque drive. You may stop for a relaxing Southern-style breakfast, lunch, or dinner at the **Green Shutters Inn** (706–782–3342), a pretty little place with an antiques shop upstairs from the dining room, between Clayton and the community of Tiger.

The Clayton Welcome Center (706–782–5113), on Highway 441, can give you further tips on off-the-beaten-path adventures. You may also contact the Rabun County Chamber of Commerce, Box 761, Clayton 30525, (706) 782–4812.

It may be difficult to imagine now, but early in this century, **Tallulah Falls** was one of the South's most popular summer resorts. Honeymooners, families, and other nature-loving city folk came to admire the cataracts of the Tallulah River, which stormed through a gorge 820 feet across and more than 1,200 feet deep. All that ended in the early 1920s, when a series of hydroelectric dams diverted water from the falls but at the same time created Lake Rabun, Lake Burton, and other recreational areas.

◆ **Tallulah Gorge Park and Terrora Park and Camp-**

ground, one of the newest state parks, invites hikers to explore the depths of the gorge. The parks department and Georgia Power Company plan to return the falls to their thundering glory. The Terrora Park area has a fishing pier and picnic tables on the Tallulah River. Exhibits explain Georgia Power's conservation efforts. Fifty campsites have water and electrical hookups. Phone (800) 864–PARK for reservations. If you'd like to hike the gorge, you'll need to register, free of charge, at the visitors center by the Highway 441 bridge. For general information contact Park Superintendent, P.O. Box 248, Tallulah Falls 30573, (706) 754–8257 or 754–6036.

Tallulah Gallery (706–754–6020) has a beautiful selection of paintings, pottery, weaving, and other mountain handicrafts in the parlors of a Victorian mansion built by the president of the now-extinct local railroad. The two-story home is on Highway 441 in the center of the small community. Open daily.

Traveling on Highway 441 between Tallulah Falls and Clayton, Dillard, and Mountain City, you'll be sorely tempted by a raft of mountain-craft shops and art galleries. **Lofty Branch Art and Craft Village,** 6 miles south of Clayton, (706) 782–5246, is a scattered complex of studios offering mostly high-quality weaving, woodwork, leather, pottery, and glass.

Green thumbers shouldn't miss a visit to ❖ **Penny's Garden.** Look for a small sign at Highway 441 and Darling Springs Road, north of the entrance to Black Rock Mountain State Park. Follow a winding road to Penny and Don Melton's greenhouse and shop. There you can purchase fresh flowers (you can pick your own), herbs, gourmet jams and vinegars, baskets, garden ornaments, birdhouses, sachets and potpourris, and gourmet herbal foods. You can also sign up for gardening or herbal workshops. Write P.O. Box 305, Blacks Creek Road, Mountain City 30562, or call (706) 746–6918.

The ❖ **Foxfire Museum,** on Highway 441, 3 miles north of Clayton, (706) 746–5828, is a treat for all those who've enjoyed the long series of *Foxfire Books.* The books—in case you're not familiar with them—chronicle the research by students at Rabun Gap-Nacoochee School who were sent into the hills to preserve their endangered heritage. The small museum displays furniture, baskets, logging and woodworking tools, animal traps, farm implements, part of a gristmill, and other necessities of nineteenth- and early twentieth-century Appalachian life. Admission

137

is free, but donations are always welcome.

For the ultimate in rustic mountain lodgings and some of Georgia's most accomplished home cooking, head for **LaPrade's,** a cluster of cabins, a dining room, and fishing docks on Highway 197 at Lake Burton. Built in the early 1920s, the spartan pine cabins have full kitchens and bathrooms and sleep up to twelve. Meals are served family-style, all-you-can-eat, at long communal tables in the screened-in dining room.

Breakfast is highlighted by country ham and sausage, hot biscuits and sorghum syrup, and grits and eggs. Chicken and dumplings, barbecue, meat loaf, vegetables, and corn bread are served at weekday lunch. Some of the world's finest Southern fried chicken is the centerpiece of Sunday lunch and weekday dinner.

You may have all those meals, and your cabin, for $36 a person a day; ages 3 to 9 are half-price; under age 3, free. If you're just dropping by at mealtime, breakfast is $6.75, lunch $8.75, dinner and Sunday lunch $10.75. Again, children 3 to 9 are half-price and those under age 3 are free. The dining room is closed Tuesday and Wednesday. Contact LaPrade's, Highway 197 north, Clarkesville 30523, (706) 947–3312 and (800) 262–3313 for "The Meal Reservation Hot Line."

Beechwood Inn Bed & Breakfast, P.O. Box 120, Clayton 30525, (706) 782–5485, is one of the mountain country's newest and nicest small lodgings. Innkeeper Marty Lott fastidiously restored this old Rabun County summer vacation house, originally built in 1922. On a rise, among terraced gardens, the house has dramatic views of the neighboring mountains. Five guest rooms have queen-size or twin beds. All have their own baths, and some have working fireplaces. Marty sends you off in the morning with an excellent full breakfast. The location is especially convenient to launching points for Chattooga River rafting adventures. Moderate rates are seasonal.

Two scenic state parks in Rabun County offer a wealth of outdoor activities and overnight lodgings. ◆ **Black Rock Mountain State Park,** 1,500 acres of brawny beauty atop a 3,600-foot elevation of the Blue Ridge Mountains, has an eighteen-acre lake, many miles of wooded nature trails, waterfalls, and campsites with electrical and water hookups and kitchens. Contact Park Superintendent, Black Rock Mountain, P.O. Drawer A, Mountain City 30562; (706) 746–2141.

◆ **Moccasin Creek State Park,** on Lake Burton, has a boat ramp and docks, a trout hatchery, hiking trails, and campsites. For reservations phone (800) 864–PARK. Contact Park Superintendent, Moccasin Creek State Park, Route 1, Box 1634, Clarkesville 30523; (706) 947–3194.

For twelve days early every August, the normally unhurried Towns County seat of Hiawassee (population 1,985) throbs with the energy of the ◆ **Georgia Mountain Fair.** Against a backdrop of Blue Ridge Mountains, forests, and blue-green lakes, the fair takes Hiawassee and the rest of Georgia's **"Little Switzerland"** literally by storm.

The fairgrounds resound with the music of bluegrass fiddlers, gospel singers, clog dancers, and some of the very big names of the country music entertainment world. Scores of craftsmen show off their skills at woodworking, pottery, cornshuck and applehead dolls, painting, leatherwork, furniture and toy making, jewelry, basket weaving, needlework, quilting, and macramé.

Pioneer Village is like a walk through a mountain town of yesteryear. You can peruse the canned goods and bolt cloth in the mercantile store, see the hickory switch in the one-room schoolhouse, visit the smokehouse, and stop in at the hand-hewn log cabin. Elsewhere on the forty-two-acre grounds, you can taste just-squeezed apple cider and see a "moonshine" whiskey still up close. "Revenooers" keep a close guard against any free samples. For information contact Towns County Chamber of Commerce, 1140 Fuller Court, Hiawassee 30546, (706) 896–4966.

From early June to early August you can enjoy **"The Reach of Song."** Georgia's official state historic drama tells the story of the mountain folk with fiddling, gospel singing, dancing, tale swapping, and problem sharing. It's performed in a new house on the Young Harris College Campus, Young Harris 30582, (800) 262–7664.

Most of the year **Lake Chatuge** is a great place to play. The 7,500-acre Tennessee Valley Authority (TVA) reservoir on the western edge of the Hiawassee is a tranquil retreat for trout and bass fishermen, waterskiers, swimmers, and boaters. Several marinas and public boat docks offer easy access to the lake. You'll also find picnic grounds, tennis courts, a sand beach, playgrounds, and camping sites at the 160-acre **Towns County Park** on the lakeside.

139

The ◆ **Chattahoochee National Forest** blankets much of Towns County with Georgia pines and hardwoods. Sections of four national wilderness areas in the county afford you the opportunity to get well off the beaten track. During certain times of the year, the Appalachian Trail, crossing Towns County near Brasstown Bald Mountain, gets downright busy as hikers test their stamina on the 2,000-mile Maine-to-Georgia route described at the beginning of this chapter.

At **Brasstown Bald Mountain**—see Russell-Brasstown Scenic Byway—you may follow the 5½-mile Arkaquah Trail from the crest of Trackrock Gap and the less-strenuous 2½-mile Jack's Trail Knob to the foot of Brasstown. Wagon Train Road meanders 6 miles to a pastoral valley that cradles the pretty town of Young Harris and the campus of Young Harris College.

A short drive from Brasstown Bald Mountain, **7 Creeks Housekeeping Cabins,** is an answered prayer for anyone who's ever dreamt of "getting away from it all." In the midst of gorgeous mountain scenery, the seven cabins, sleeping four to eight, are completely furnished except for bed linens, which can be rented for a modest charge. All have baths, full kitchens, grills, and picnic tables. You can swim and fish in a private lake, pet farm animals, and play badminton and horseshoes. Rates of $33 to $53 daily, $235 to $275 weekly for one to two persons, $5 a day for each additional person. Contact 7 Creeks, Route 2, Box 2647, Blairsville 30512, (706) 745-4753

◆ **Brasstown Valley Crowne Plaza Resort,** opened in 1995 on a scenic 503-acre Blue Ridge mountainscape, has all the upscale resort bells and whistles: 134 attractively appointed guest rooms in the four-story main lodge and adjacent cottages; 18-hole, 7,000-yard Scottish links–style golf course; and tennis, horseshoes, trout fishing, horseback riding, indoor/outdoor pool, fitness center, and full-service restaurant and lounge. It's a great place to roost for a while and an excellent base while sightseeing in the surrounding mountainlands. Lodge rooms run $119–$149, cottages $129–$149 per bedroom. Brasstown Resort is in Young Harris 30582, (706) 379–9900.

Deer Lodge, a hideaway near the junction of Highways 66 and 75, is another heaven-sent place to park a while and savor the glories of the mountains. Hospitable proprietors Richard and Willene Haigler serve some of the biggest, best, and lowest-priced steaks and trout anywhere in these parts. Cabins secluded in the nearby woods are $25 a night for two persons and $45 for four. Contact Deer Lodge, Hiawassee 30546, 9706) 896–2726.

The ❖ **Russell-Brasstown Scenic Byway,** in White and Union Counties, takes you through the heart of some of northeast Georgia's most spectacular mountain country. Designated as Highway 348, the 14-mile paved highway takes you from the outskirts of Georgia's "Alpine Village" of Helen, across the Appalachian Trail, to the state's highest mountain and a picture postcard state park. Several parking areas and overlooks give you the chance to stop and admire the rugged beauty of the Blue Ridge Mountains. The drive is especially striking in mid-October to early November, when the hardwoods turn brilliantly orange, yellow, and scarlet.

One of the Scenic Highway's "high points" is 3,137-foot **Tesnatee Gap,** where the Appalachian Trail crosses on its way between Maine and Springer Mountain, Georgia. You can get out of your car here and mingle a while with the earnest hikers. At its northwestern end the Scenic Highway intersects with Highway 180. If you turn right, you may explore 4,784-foot Brasstown Bald. A steep, paved road ends at a parking area 930 feet below the summit. From here either hike to the crest of Georgia's highest peak or take a commercial van up to the view of four states.

A left turn at Highway 180 will lead you to Highway 19 and ❖ **Vogel State Park.** Cradled in mountains, beside a pretty lake, Vogel is a delightful place for fishing, boating, warm weather swimming, and year-round hiking on woodland trails. The park's seventy-two campsites have electricity, water, hot showers, and rest rooms; thirty-six rustic but very snug cottages, by the lake and in the adjacent woodlands, are equipped down to sheets, towels, pots, and pans. For reservations phone (800) 864–PARK. The park also has a $2.00 one-time parking fee. The park office is open 8:00 A.M. to 5:00 P.M. Contact Vogel State Park, Blairsville 30512, (706) 745–2628.

Georgia Highway 180, which joins U.S. Highway 19 north of Vogel Park, is a 22-mile scenic mountain route to the little community of Suches. Along the way stop at **Sosebee Cove Scenic Area,** where a half-mile loop trail takes you through a second growth forest with wildflowers and rhododendron. Farther along ❖ **Lake Winfield Scott Recreation Area** has a thirty-two-acre campground with showers ($6.00 a night) and an eighteen-acre fishing and swimming lake. There is a $2.00 parking fee for noncampers.

Habersham County claims some of northeast Georgia's most photogenic Blue Ridge Mountain country. These mountains and valleys, thousands of acres of Chattahoochee National Forest, and scores of lakes and streams offer limitless opportunities to take a hike, ride a bike, camp out, and fish, swim, and otherwise unwind.

Habersham is one of Georgia's major apple producers. Rich soil and a cool climate encouraged English and Canadian families to initiate the apple-growing arts here in the 1920s. In October, roadside stands overflow with Red Delicious, Stayman Winesaps, dark red Yates, and bright yellow-green Granny Smiths. You can buy 'em by the sackful or the carload and also purchase homemade apple jelly, apple butter, and ice-cold, freshly squeezed sweet apple cider by the glass and gallon jugful. As a rule Habersham owners don't allow visitors to come in and pick their own fruit.

Habersham County also produces enough grapes to merit location of one of Georgia's major wineries. ❖ **Habersham Vineyards** (706–778–WINE) at Highways 365 and 441 near the small town of Baldwin, produces more than a dozen types of wine, including pinot blanc, Chablis, chardonnay, Riesling, and sauvignon. Habersham's Georgia muscadine wine has won gold medals in international competitions. Other wines have captured silver and bronze medals here and overseas.

You may tour the winery and enjoy free samples Monday through Saturday 10:00 A.M. to 5:00 P.M. and Sunday 1:00 to 6:00 P.M.

Clarkesville, Habersham's snug little county seat, is a happy hunting ground for antiques and mountain handicrafts. Several shops around the courthouse square on Highway 441 are loaded with handcrafted furniture, pottery, paintings, weaving, leatherwork, handmade baskets and quilts, toys, dolls, jellies, jams, and preserves.

When all that browsing and decision making saps your strength, go for a recharge at **Taylor's Trolley** (706–754–5566), a turn-of-the-century drugstore turned into a most attractive cafe. Owners Turi and Ron Nixon have re-created the old soda fountain feeling with ceiling fans, country antiques, and old-timey chairs and tables. The service area is behind the marble soda fountain. The menu includes fresh mountain trout, steaks, prime rib, homemade soups, salads, sandwiches, and desserts. Prices are inexpensive at lunch Monday through Saturday, and dinner Tuesday through Saturday. Taylor's Trolley is located on Highway 441 at the town square, Clarkesville 30523.

The **Glen-Ella Springs Hotel** sits on seventeen pastoral acres, off Highway 441/23 between Clarkesville and Tallulah Falls. Owners Barrie and Bobby Aycock have converted the one-hun-dred-year-old hotel building into a sixteen-room country inn, full of rustic touches and modern conveniences. In warm weather, enjoy the outdoor swimming pool. All the rooms have porches with rocking chairs, antiques, and heart-of-pine panel-ing. Some have fireplaces and whirlpools. The dining room fea-tures fresh mountain trout but varies from traditional mountain fare with veal dishes, pasta, scallops, fresh fish, and other Ameri-can/continental entrees. Doubles are $80–$150, including full breakfast. Contact the Aycocks, Route 3, Bear Gap Road, Clarkesville 30523, (706) 754–7295.

Highway 197, twisting and turning north between Clarkesville and Clayton, is considered one of north Georgia's prettiest drives. The ❖ **Mark of the Potter,** 9 miles north of Clarkesville, is a favorite stop for mountain visitors. The weath-ered old white frame corn-grinding mill, by the rapids of the Soque River, sells some of the finest work of Georgia's most accomplished craftspeople. Shelves are laden with superb pot-tery, colorful fabrics, metal, and leatherwork.

Browsing inevitably will take you onto the porch overhanging the Soque to throw treats to the fat, pampered trout swimming in the river's pools. Mark of the Potter (706–947–3440) is open daily. If you follow Highway 197 another 8 miles north, you'll be at the dining room of LaPrade's, one of the mountains' most famous eateries (see page 138). Habersham also shares Tallulah Falls and Tallulah Gorge with Rabun County.

South of Clarkesville, the little town of **Demorest,** on High-way 441, is worth a visit. A couple of antiques shops are on the short main street, and you may stroll through the peaceful cam-pus of Piedmont College.

When your children pose that age-old question—"Where do babies come from?"—take them to Cleveland and show them. At Cleveland's ❖ **Babyland General Hospital** (706–865–2171) some very special "babies" come from a cabbage patch. Origi-nally a doctor's turn-of-the-century clinic, the white frame "hos-

143

pital" at 19 Underwood Street/Highway 129 is where the soft-sculpted Cabbage Patch Kids, created by White County's own Xavier Roberts's, first see day's light. Uniformed "nurses" lead you through the nursery, day-care center, and delivery room. At the magic moment, a "doctor" in surgical garb plucks a new-born Kid from a patch of sculpted cabbage leaves to "oohs" and "aahs" all around. You can take home a cuddly Cabbage Patch Kid of your very own. Just remember, they're "babies," not "dolls"; not "bought," but "adopted." The hospital is open Monday through Saturday 8:30 A.M. to 5:00 P.M. and Sunday 1:00 to 5:00 P.M.

Xavier Roberts's rich imagination has created the Blue Ridge country's most exotic, and unusual, lodgings. Departing totally from traditional mountain architecture, **Villagio di Montagna** seems more like a French or Italian import. Nestled among the trees and hills, Villagio's Mediterranean/art deco buildings are a muted mauve color, with ample use of tiles, marble, and glass blocks. Guest rooms have service bars and refrigerators, private balconies, fireplaces, and satellite television. Guests may while away their days at the swimming pool, tropical gardens, a rock garden Jacuzzi, and a spa with whirlpool, steam room, and sauna. Doubles are $80 to $450 (for the three-story lodge sleeping eighteen). Contact P.O. Box 714, Cleveland 30528, (706) 865–7000 and (800) 367–3922.

Cleveland's town square has lots of places to buy pottery, weaving, paintings, and other mountain handicrafts. For a taste of the mountains, head for **Ma Gooch's** (706–865–2023), a cafe and social center where locals meet to eat and exchange the day's news over daily breakfast, lunch, and dinner. It's in front of the Gateway Motel at Highways 192 and 17.

If the sheer granite escarpments of **Mount Yonah,** off Highway 75 north of Cleveland, set your rock-climbing juices flowing, make plans to scale the heights with commercial outfitters in Atlanta. High Country Outfitters (404–434–7578) will put you in the proper climbing gear and send you up Yonah's 150- to 300-foot cliffs with experienced guides. Mount Yonah is also one of Georgia's best and most popular hang-gliding points.

Driving up to the ◆ **Old Sautee Store** (706–878–2281) at the junction of Highways 17 and 255, you might imagine an old-time mercantile stocked with bolts of cloth, seeds, farm implements, and sacks of cornmeal. Walk inside and what do your wondering eyes behold, but an array of tempting goods from Scandinavia: Norwegian and Icelandic sweaters, jackets, and coats; crystal, dinnerware, needlework, gourmet foods, jewelry, and unique gifts from Sweden, Denmark, and Finland. On special occasions, owner Astrid Fried appears in her ornate Norwegian wedding dress. The adjacent log cabin sells Christmas ornaments year-round. The store is open daily.

Just down Highway 255 west from the store, jog down an unpaved lane past horse and cattle farms, and come to rest at **Lumsden Homeplace.** The sturdy white farmhouse was built in 1890 by the great-grandparents of Mike Crittenden, who now runs it as a country inn with his wife, Linda. Five large guest rooms have period furnishings, family mementos, and private baths. The Crittendens send you off in the morning with a memorable mountain breakfast. Doubles are $65. Write P.O. Box 388, Highway 255, Sautee-Nacoochee 30571; or phone (706) 878–2813.

You can also spread a picnic by the ❖ **Stovall Covered Bridge,** in a small park by Chickamauga Creek on Highway 255. Only 33 feet long, the bridge is one of the shortest anywhere in Georgia.

The **Stovall House,** nearby on Highway 255, is one of the nicest country inns anywhere in the state. Built in 1837, the handsome two-story frame house was purchased in 1982 by former Atlantan Ham Schwartz. His love of his adopted mountain home is reflected in five guest rooms decorated with country antiques and all the modern comforts. The dining room features Southern and continental cooking and is one of the best anywhere in the mountains. For pure, sweet relaxation, settle yourself into a porch swing and listen to the absolute peace of this lovely countryside. Rates are about $63 weekdays, $70 weekends, for a double. Contact the Stovall House, Route 1, Box 103-A, Sautee 30571, (706) 878–3355.

Highway 17 cuts a most picturesque path through the Sautee-Nacoochee Valley as it meanders westerly toward Helen. You may want to stop for a picture—or attend Sunday services—at **Crescent Hill Baptist Church,** on a wooded hillock near the intersection of Highways 17 and 75. The pretty Carpenter Gothic church was built in the 1870s by the same well-off gentleman who built the grand Victorian house and gazebo atop the Indian mound at Highways 17 and 75.

Going north on combined Highway 17/75, stop off at **Nora Mill Granary & Store** (706–878–2927). Founded in 1876 on the banks of the Chattahoochee River, the mill's current owners still grind corn into meal and grits in the tried and true old-fashioned way. It's open daily.

Don't try to pinch yourself awake as you drive by the "Wilkommen" signs welcoming you to ◈ **"Alpine Helen."** You haven't wandered onto a Disney film set. About twenty years ago this then-humble mountain hamlet underwent a wholesale transformation into a make-believe Alpine village. Nowadays, the red-tile roofs, flower boxes, biergartens, and stucco-fronted shops selling cuckoo clocks, Christmas ornaments, Tyrolean hats, and loden coats put the once-quiet village very much on the well-beaten path. Like it or disdain it, Helen's worth at least a short stroll and a browse. The many inns and "hofs" around town are good bases for more off-the-beaten-path adventures, such as the Appalachian Trail, Russell-Brasstown Scenic Byway, and Chattahoochee National Forest. In trout season, you can don your waders and cast in the Chattahoochee River, which rises near here and wends its bonny way through the middle of town.

More Blue Ridge than Bavarian, **Betty's Country Store** (706–878–2943), on the north end of town, is a fun place to look around. The rustic store is loaded with jams and jellies, fresh vegetables, gourds, cookbooks, canned goods, cheeses, gourmet coffee, apple cider, and other goods. The cafe area in the back serves a hearty breakfast and great chili, sandwiches, and desserts. It's open every day.

If you've never made it to Munich for Oktoberfest, Helen has a scaled-down replica. In late September and early October, the town's pavilion resounds to oompah bands and thousands of folk-dancing feet. In late October and early November, the mountain hardwoods change their colors as brilliantly as those in New England, making this an especially worthwhile time to visit. It's also prime season for freshly squeezed apple cider and boiled peanuts. Simmered in brine, in huge iron kettles, the goobers are warm, salty, sticky, and a special mountain delicacy that not everyone goes for, but that should at least be experienced.

◈ **Unicoi State Park,** just north of Helen, is a treat that everyone can enjoy. With 1,081 acres of highlands and woodlands, threaded by streams, lakes, and waterfalls, there's plenty of off-the-beaten-path solitude.

Swimming, canoeing, and fishing focus on a picture-postcard fifty-three-acre lake. You may take solitary walks on 12 miles of trails and take part in nature walks led by park naturalists. Craftsmen share the secrets of pottery, quilting, dulcimer- and furniture-making, and other mountain arts. The handicraft shop in the Unicoi Lodge sells an array of beautiful items.

Also in the lodge the cafeteria-style dining room serves excellent breakfast, lunch, and dinner at extremely low prices. The park's accommodations include ninety-six camping sites, with water, electricity, nearby showers, and rest rooms; and two- and three-bedroom, completely furnished cottages. For reservations call (800) 864–PARK. Contact Park Superintendent, P.O. Box 849, Helen 30545, (706) 878–2201.

❧ **Anna Ruby Falls** is the awesome showpiece of a 1,600-acre Cattahoochee National Forest recreation area that neighbors Unicoi. From the parking area follow a moderately strenuous half-mile trail through the woodlands bordering a swift-flowing stream. An observation platform sits at the base of Anna Ruby's two cascades, dropping dramatically 153 and 50 feet over the edge of Tray Mountain. Back at the parking area, restore your energy with a picnic by the water's edge. A handsome new visitors center has an excellent gift shop and a porch from which you can toss treats to some of creation's fattest trout. A Trail for the Blind identifies trees and plants in Braille. There is a $2.00 per car parking fee.

In 1828 a trapper named Benjamin Parks allegedly stubbed his toe on a rock in Dahlonega and shouted the north Georgia version of "Eureka!" as he gazed at a vein of gold that soon sent prospectors streaming into these hills. *Dahlonega* is a Cherokee Indian word meaning "precious yellow," and until the War Between the States, the substance flowed into a major U.S. Mint right here. Although it's no longer a major industry, enough gold is still mined to periodically releaf the dome of Georgia's state capitol and intrigue visitors who pan for it at reconstructed camps.

True to its heritage, the ❧ **Dahlonega Courthouse Gold Museum,** in the center of the little town of 2,800, chronicles the gold rush and the numerous mines that flourished in these parts. A twenty-eight-minute film upstairs in the old courtroom is especially worthwhile. Operated by the Georgia Department of Natural Resources, the Gold Museum, Dahlonega 30533, (706) 864–2257, is open Tuesday through Saturday 9:00 A.M. to 5:00

147

P.M. and Sunday 2:00 to 5:30 P.M. Adults are $2.00; ages 6 to 18, $1.00; under age 5, no charge.

Buildings around the square have a rustic frontier look. Shops purvey gold-panning equipment, ice cream, fudge, mountain handicrafts, gold jewelry, and antiques. Many people make the 70-mile drive north from Atlanta just to feast at the famous **Smith House.** It's off the square at 202 South Chestatee Street, Dahlonega 30533, (706) 864–3566. The Smith House puts out huge family-style spreads with fried chicken, chicken and dumplings, beef stew, shrimp, numerous vegetables, biscuits, relishes, and dessert for about $12 a person. They also serve breakfast and have a cafeteria line for those not up to the full board. It's open daily except Monday.

For something lighter and trendier, go for pasta, seafood, and chicken dishes at **Nature's Cellar,** (706–864–6829). This cozy dark-paneled cafe is across from the Gold Museum.

The **Worley Homestead Inn,** at 410 West Main Street, Dahlonega 30533, (706) 864–7002, is a short stroll from the Gold Museum, restaurants, and shops on Dahlonega's square. Seven guest rooms in the mid-nineteenth-century Victorian house are full of antiques and pictures of Worley family ancestors. Each has a private bath, some with claw-foot tubs. There are even rumors of a friendly resident haint. The $65–$85 tariff qualifies you for a huge country breakfast.

Mountain Top Lodge has a wealth of creature comforts including air-conditioning, contemporary-country furnishings, private baths, and outdoor patios. An outdoor hot tub eases the aches of a hard day on the craft-shopping trail. Doubles, with a huge breakfast, are $55 to $125. Located down a winding farm road and atop a wooded hilltop 5 miles southwest of the Dahlonega square, the Mountain Top has thirteen guest rooms in its main lodge and adjacent cottage. Route 7, Box 150, Dahlonega 30533; or phone (706) 864–5257.

Gold Rush Days, the third weekend of October, celebrates the gilded heritage with arts and crafts, clog dancing, and lots of bluegrass fiddling and singing. You can pan for gold year-round at **Crisson's Mine,** Wimpy Mill Road, Dahlonega 30533. You'll feel some of old Benjamin Park's excitement and might even whoop out "Eureka!" when you spot a few grains gleaming amid the mud in your pan. Phone (706) 864–6363.

You can also take a guided walk through the tunnels of the

old **Consolidated Mine.** At the turn of the century, it was the largest and richest gold mine in the Eastern United States. It went mysteriously bankrupt in 1906, and much of the old equipment is still in place. Phone (706) 864–8473.

Dahlonega is a popular gateway to the northeast Georgia mountain vacation areas. From here Highway 19 snakes north toward Vogel State Park, while other roads aim toward Helen, Cleveland, and Amicalola State Park.

Contact Dahlonega–Lumpkin County Chamber of Commerce, 101 South Park Street, Dahlonega 30533, (706) 864–3711.

Two of north Georgia's most interesting and unusual dining and lodging places are off the beaten path among the green hills and marble quarries of Pickens County. The Woodbridge Inn at Jasper and the Tate House at Tate depart joyously and deliciously from the culinary path most often trod in rural Georgia.

German-born Joe Rueffert and his Georgia-born wife Brenda have been the hospitable proprietors of the **Woodbridge Inn** for about a dozen years. On the surface, the rustic pre–Civil War inn, with the checkered tablecloths and big windows with panoramic views of the mountains, gives few hints of surprises. It's only when Joe dons his chef's hat and parades from the kitchen with grilled swordfish steaks, fresh grouper, and mahi-mahi with rich creamy sauces; chateaubriand *forestière* and steak *au poivre;* veal dishes with silken béarnaise and hollandaise sauces; roast duckling with orange sauce; bananas Foster and other luscious desserts that the wealth of this "find" finally sinks in.

You may select American or European wines and beers from the Woodbridge list. After your feast, you're only a few steps from your lodgings in the inn's chalet-style rooms. Comfortably furnished and air-conditioned, the large rooms come with complimentary mountain views for $50 to $70. The dining room serves lunch on Sunday and dinner Tuesday through Saturday. Prices are moderate, and major credit cards are accepted. Contact Woodbridge Inn, 411 Chambers Street, Jasper 30143, (706) 692–6293.

The inn is, true to its name, across a wooden bridge, at the northern edge of the bucolic small town of Jasper. If you've forgotten how sweet and peaceful a town of 5,000 can be, take a leisurely constitutional on Jasper's main street, and chat with the folks in the stores and around the Pickens County Courthouse. The Ruefferts don't serve breakfast, so you may wish to indulge in the grits and eggs at one of Jasper's hometown cafes.

A driving tour of Pickens County is a nice way to spend a day. **John's Mill,** a nineteenth-century water-powered mill, is a picturesque place to picnic and to buy a sackful of stone-ground cornmeal. From the junction of Highway 53 and I–575, drive west on Highway 53 about 7 miles and turn right on the road between the Hinton Milling Co. and a service station. Continue ¼-mile to the John's Mill sign and turn left; the log cabin mill and stone dam are at the bottom of the hill. There's no phone, but the mill is usually in operation on weekdays and Saturdays.

◆ **Amicalola Falls State Park** and the **Appalachian Trail approach trail** are a scenic half-hour drive from Jasper, in neighboring Dawson County. The 400-acre park, centered on a majestic 729-foot waterfall has hiking trails above and below the falls, picnic areas, fishing, campsites—with electricity, water, hot showers, and rest rooms—and furnished cottages with fireplaces. The handsome **Amicalola Falls Lodge** has fifty-seven guest rooms with spectacular views and all the modern comforts. For reservations phone (800) 864–PARK. Contact the park at Star Route, Box 215, Dawsonville 30534, (706) 265–8888. The Appalachian Trail is described at the beginning of this chapter.

The mountain may not have come to Mohammed, as the old saying goes, but in 1957, an inland sea came to northeast Georgia's Hall County. The U.S. Army Corps of Engineers closed the Buford Dam on the Chattahoochee River and created Lake Sidney Lanier. Nowadays about 25,000 of the lake's 38,000 acres and some 380 miles of its green and hilly 550-mile shoreline cover former Hall County farmlands and forests.

◆ **Lake Lanier Islands** is the huge waterway's biggest recreational package. Developed by the state on wooded hilltops that bobbed above the water after the dam was closed, the islands have a lifeguarded, Florida-sand swimming beach; an 850,000-gallon wave pool; mild and hair-raising water slides; miniature golf and championship golf; all kinds of rental boats, such as houseboats, pontoon boats, sport boats, ski boats, sailboats, fishing boats, and paddle boats; horseback riding; picnic grounds; campgrounds; and two deluxe resort hotels. **Stouffer PineIsle Resort** (770–945–8921) has 250 guest rooms, three restaurants, indoor and outdoor tennis, and an indoor/outdoor swimming pool. Stoufffer PineIsle Resort Golf Course wraps 8 of its 18 holes around the lakeshore. **Lake Lanier Islands Hilton Resort** (770–945–8787), with 224 guest rooms and full amenities, invites guests and nonguests to challenge its par-72 championship-style golf course.

While you're admiring the scenery, beware of thirteen water holes! The Islands's 300 lakeside campsites are equipped with water, electricity, and some sewer hookups. Campers also have their own fishing pier, outdoor pavilion, and boat launch ramp. For reservations phone (770) 932–7270. Admission to the Islands is $4.00 a car for one day, $16.00 for a year. All facilities, including the swimming beach, are extra. For information contact **Lake Lanier Islands,** 6950 Holiday Road, Lake Lanier Islands 30518 (770) 932–7200; and **Gainesville-Hall County Convention and Visitors Bureau,** 830 Green Street, Gainesville 30501, (770) 536–5209.

At the end of a big day of fishing, boating, and swimming, join famished natives at **Major McGill's Fish House,** an unpretentious and always busy set of dining rooms in the small community of Flowery Branch, just off Highway 13, (770) 967–6001. Specialties are fried and broiled Lake Lanier catfish, oysters, shrimp, mountain trout, steaks, and chicken.

Gainesville, the Hall County seat (population about 40,000), is a popular gateway to the northeast Georgia vacationlands. Before heading for the hills, enjoy a leisurely stroll through the **Green Street Historical District.** The wide, tree-lined thoroughfare, also designated as Highway 129, holds a wealth of late nineteenth- and early twentieth-century Victorian and Neoclassical Revival residences. **Rudolph's On Green Street,** 700 Green Street, (770) 534–2226, is a baronial English Tudor rich with dark, exposed beams, stained-glass windows, Oriental carpets, and Duncan Phyfe furnishings. Lunch and dinner entrees are equally impressive: broiled baby salmon, chicken Florentine, roast duckling, several veal dishes, and Georgia mountain trout complemented by wines from California, Georgia, and Europe. You may also have a hamburger, salads, and a simple breakfast or eggs Benedict. Prices range from inexpensive to expensive and major credit cards are accepted. Lunch Monday through Friday, dinner Monday through Saturday.

Poor Richard's, 1702 Parkhill Drive, (770) 532–0499, has been Gainesville's choice for steaks, prime rib, chateaubriand, baby back ribs, shrimp, lobster, and chicken since 1977. They'll also serve you a hefty hamburger, salads, sandwiches, and wine. Dinner is served Monday to Saturday.

The Dunlap House Bed & Breakfast Inn, at 635 Green Street, Gainesville 30501, (770) 536–0200, is another gracious Green Street landmark. Built in 1910, the ten-room mansion was turned into a luxury bed-and-breakfast in 1985. Each uniquely decorated guest room has either a queen- or king-size bed, a private bath, telephone, TV, designer linens, oversize towels, and terry cloth robes. Some rooms have working fireplaces. Continental breakfast is included in the $85 to $120 tariff.

Whitworth Inn Bed & Breakfast, at 6593 McEver Road, Flowery Branch 30542, (770) 967–2386, has ten light, airy guest rooms, all with private baths, a few minutes from Lake Lanier. Enjoy the cool mountain air on open porches. Innkeepers Ken and Christine Jonick send you off in the morning with a full country breakfast. Doubles are $59, singles $55.

Also in the Green Street Historical District, the **Quinlan Art Center** (770–536–2575) shows the works of state, regional, and national artists Monday through Saturday 10:00 A.M. to 4:00 P.M. and Sundays 2:00 to 5:00 P.M. at no charge.

The ◆ **Georgia Mountains Museum,** 311 Green Street, (770) 536–0889, fills an old two-story fire station with history and memorabilia of Georgia's hardy mountainfolk. One of the most popular exhibits is the "Ed Dodd Room," dedicated to the Gainesville native son who created the "Mark Trail" comic strip adventurer. You'll also see excellent displays on Native Americans, Black history, textiles, Gainesville's vital poultry industry, spinning, weaving, and pioneer life. Two blocks from the main museum, the affiliated **Railroad Museum** houses memorabilia in a renovated baggage car. Open Tuesday to Saturday. Free admission.

◆ **Elachee Nature Science Center,** at 2125 Elachee Drive, (770) 535–2302, is a great place to get lost in the woods for a while and learn something about the world around us. The heavily wooded, 1,200-acre preserve's many fascinating experiences include please-touch fish, amphibians, reptiles, and a 300-gallon trout tank. The interactive, computer, and contemporary music–enhanced "If Everyone Lived Like Me" exhibit looks at the effects of our lifestyles on our environment. Enjoy the tranquil beauty of the Chicopee Woods Nature Preserve on 2.5 miles of nature trails, where you can take a close look at animal and plant habitats. Open Monday to Saturday. Adults are $3.00; children, $1.50.

All the buildings around **Roosevelt Square,** in the center of Gainesville, have a distinctive 1930s art deco look. That's because all the older buildings in the area were lost, along with many lives, in a monster tornado in 1936. President Franklin D. Roosevelt's "New Deal" programs rebuilt the devastated town, and he spoke here at dedication ceremonies in 1938.

If you enjoy unusual monuments, bring your camera to **Poultry Park,** where a rooster atop a granite obelisk hails Gainesville's distinction as "Poultry Capital of the World." Some 2.6-million broilers leave here every week for kitchens around the world.

WINERIES AND BIG LAKES

Created by U.S. Army Corps of Engineers impoundments of the Savannah River, **Lake Hartwell** is a vast inland sea, whose 56,000 acres offer virtually limitless off-the-beaten-path opportunities for fishing, boating, swimming, and nature hikes. You can headquarter at two state parks on the lake and play a 9-hole golf course at another park, away from the lake. While wandering the green and hilly backroads of Hart, Stephens, and Franklin Counties, you can rest a while at an eighteenth-century stagecoach inn and reminisce with old-timers who remember the fiery exploits of "The Georgia Peach," baseball's Ty Cobb.

◆ **Hart State Park,** near the town of Hartwell, spreads 147 acres along the lakeshore. You can set up housekeeping in eighty-three tent trailer sites, with electrical and water hookups, adjacent to showers and rest rooms, and in furnished cottages. For reservations phone (800) 864–PARK. You can indulge in swimming, boating, waterskiing, and fishing for largemouth bass, black crappie, bream, rainbow trout, and walleye pike. You can angle from fishing docks or find your own favorite spot away from the competition. Contact Park Superintendent, 1515 Hart Park Road, Hartwell 30643, (706) 376–8756.

Situated on a wooded peninsula jutting into Lake Hartwell, ◆ **Tugaloo State Park,** near Lavonia, is another motherlode of largemouth bass and other fish fry favorites. Nonfisherfolk can play tennis and miniature golf, swim and waterski from a sand beach, and hike and bike on trails threading through the surrounding woodlands. Lodgings include twenty furnished cottages and 122 tent and trailer sites. For reservations phone (800)

864–PARK. Contact Park Superintendent, Route 1, Lavonia 30553, (706) 356–4362.

If you've been driving all day, tantalized by thoughts of a round of golf, a swim, maybe even some late-afternoon fishing, ◆ **Victoria Bryant State Park** may be the answer to your prayers. This scenic 406-acre park, off I–85 near Royston, invites you to challenge its 3,288-yard, par-34, 9-hole golf course. It's hardly a monster, but clusters of Georgia pines plus plenty of hills and water will keep you on your toes. Rental clubs and pull carts are available at the clubhouse, which also has changing rooms and showers and a snack bar with light refreshments.

Nongolfers can splash in the swimming pool and angle for bream, bass, and catfish in the stocked pond. Victoria Bryant's twenty-five camping sites have electrical and water hookups and access to showers and rest rooms. For reservations phone (800) 864–PARK. Contact Park Superintendent, Route 1, Royston 30662, (706) 245–6270.

If you're a baseball buff, drive down to **Royston** and see the little town that gave the world "The Georgia Peach." Some gloves and bats, plaques, newspaper clippings, and other memorabilia are displayed at city hall.

In the 1830s and 1840s—about a century before Ty Cobb headed for the majors—travelers suffering the bone-jarring stagecoach journey through the northeast Georgia wilderness took solace in the thought that by and by they'd reach ◆ **Travelers Rest,** near Toccoa.

The sturdy, two-story, fourteen-room plank structure was built in 1833 as the plantation home of wealthy planter Devereaux Jarrett. As more and more travelers streamed through the region, the enterprising Jarrett added onto the house and turned it into a nineteenth-century bed-and-breakfast. South Carolina statesman John C. Calhoun was once a guest, and Joseph E. Brown, Georgia's Civil War governor, spent his honeymoon here.

Maintained by the Georgia Department of Natural Resources, the fourteen rooms are still rich with four-poster beds, rocking chairs, vanities, marble-topped tables, goose feather mattresses, spinning wheels, china, cutlery and glassware, and memorabilia of Travelers Rest's days as a post office. The grounds are shaded by a huge white oak tree, believed to be well into its third century, and several one-hundred-year-old crepe myrtles.

Off Highway 123, 6 miles northeast of Toccoa, Travelers Rest (706–886–2256) is open Tuesday through Saturday 9:00 A.M. to 5:00 P.M. and Sunday 2:00 to 5:30 P.M. Adults are $2.00; ages 6 to 18, $1.00; under 6, free.

Visitors are invited to relax by ❖ **Toccoa Falls,** a 186-foot cataract on the campus of Toccoa Falls College. A path leads to a rock wall behind the falls; another leads to a rustic stairway to the top of the falls. All is peaceful now, but on November 7, 1977, an earthen dam above the falls collapsed, sending torrents of water across the campus and claiming many lives. The dam was never replaced. The campus is on Highway 17, on the northwest side of Toccoa, a town of 10,000, near Lake Hartwell and the Georgia–South Carolina border.

Approaching the Winder/Chestnut Mountain exit (#48) on I–85 northeast of Atlanta, what appears to be a sixteenth-century French castle, surrounded by neatly laid out vineyards, rises from the piny landscape. That's no mirage. Established in the early 1980s, ❖ **Chateau Elan Winery** was Georgia's first major new winery since the end of Prohibition. Inside Chateau Elan's turreted "castle," you're welcome to stroll around a movie-set French marketplace and purchase jams, mustards, wine guides, cookbooks, picnic hampers, wine coolers, and other gifts. A pictorial display explains the history of wine and the wine-making process.

Before purchasing the chateau's grape, you'll want to have a free tasting. In a very short time, Chateau Elan's chardonnay, Riesling, cabernet sauvignon, zinfandel, and other varieties have captured more than fifty-five awards in national competitions. Southerners are especially partial to the sweet and fruity Summerwine, a blend of peaches and muscadine grapes. Wines are about $6.00 to $12.00 a bottle.

A sidewalk cafe inside the marketplace serves light lunches with quiche, pâtés, chicken breast, salads, cheeses, and Friday and Saturday evening five-course dinners with wines. You may also purchase picnic baskets and sit outdoors by the vineyards. While you're at Chateau Elan, you may also play a championship-quality golf course, walk two nature trails, and spread a picnic lunch. You may stay overnight in deluxe **Golf Villas,** and rejuvenate at the **Chateau Elan Spa,** which offers diet and nutrition services, smoking cessation programs, massages, mineral baths, herbal

155

wraps, saunas, and steam baths. Contact Chateau Elan, 7000 Old Winder Way, Braselton 30517, (770) 867–8200. The winery is open daily, free admission.

Barrow County's second winery opened in late 1988. Chestnut Mountain Winery (770–867–6914), also off I–85 exit 48, offers free tours and tastings in a farm warehouse refashioned to resemble a medieval castle. The winery is surrounded by thirty acres of woodlands and rose gardens, and visitors are welcome to bring a picnic lunch. Hours are 10:00 A.M. until dark Monday through Saturday and 12:30 to 6:00 P.M. on Sunday. Write Box 72, Braselton 30517.

◆ **Fort Yargo State Park,** at nearby Winder, takes its name from a still-standing log blockhouse that white settlers built in 1792 as protection against hostile Creeks and Cherokees. The park's big green lake is an inviting place to swim and fish and to rent paddleboats, row boats, and canoes. You can also enjoy tennis and miniature golf, hike nature trails, and set the youngsters loose on the playground. **Will-A-Way Recreation Area,** inside the park, has facilities for handicapped persons, including specially equipped, furnished cottages. There are also furnished cottages and campsites not so equipped. For reservations phone (800) 864–PARK. Contact Park Superintendent, Winder 30680, (770) 867–3489.

At Christmas season, many people bring their holiday mail to the post office in the nearby little community of Bethlehem for that special postmark.

The ◆ **Crawford W. Long Museum,** 28 College Street, (706) 367–5307, in Jefferson honors the physician who first used ether for surgical anesthesia. Dr. Long, then a young Jackson County practitioner, performed the first painless surgery on March 30, 1842. The museum displays his personal papers and a diorama depicting the first operation. An 1840s doctor's office and apothecary and a general store are also part of the museum. The outdoor herb garden grows many plants commonly used in nineteenth-century medicine. Open Tuesday to Sunday; free admission.

BULLDOG COUNTRY

Elbert County proudly hails itself "The Granite Capital of the World." The county's more than forty granite quarries and 150 monument manufacturing plants produce a third of the granite used in memorials and monuments in this country, and much of it is shipped overseas. The ❖ **Elberton Granite Museum**'s exhibits and taped programs will tell you how granite is formed, how it's quarried, the many types it comes in, and the geological differences between granite and marble. You'll also see an intriguing short film about the Georgia Guidestones. The museum is on Highway 17/77 a block from downtown Elberton. Open daily 2:00 to 5:00 P.M.; phone (706) 283–2551; free admission.

The ❖ **Georgia Guidestones,** 7 miles north of Elberton on Highway 77, may remind you of England's Stonehenge, and their origin is almost as mysterious. No one's quite certain who commissioned the Guidestones, or why. But there they are: four large granite tablets, 19 feet, 3 inches high, arranged in a spokelike pattern, with a smaller stone in the center and another across the top. Astrological readings may be made through slots and holes drilled in the stones. The Ten Commandments are etched in eight living languages, including English. Four dead languages bear this message: "Let These Be Guidestones to an Age of Reason." Other maxims inscribed on the stones include: "Be Not a Cancer on the Earth—Leave Room for Nature."

Two state parks on Savannah River reservoirs are happy hunting grounds for bass fishing. ❖ **Bobby Brown State Park,** Box 232, Elberton 30635, (706) 283–3313, has boat ramps, picnic areas, and campsites on Clarks Hill Lake. Just upriver, ❖ **Richard B. Russell State Park,** Box 118, Elberton 30635, (706) 213–3045, also has campsites, a swimming beach, boat ramps, and fish that aim to please. Both parks have $2.00 per visit parking fees. For camping reservations call (800) 864–PARK.

Antebellum Athens throbs to the contemporary rhythms of 30,000 ❖ **University of Georgia** students who nearly equal "The Classic City's" 42,000 "townies." Founded in 1785, America's oldest chartered state university didn't convene its first classes until 1801. That same year Athens was founded on a hill above the Oconee River and named for Greece's hub of classical learning. Planters and literati embellished the campus and Athens's elm- and oak-lined thoroughfares with outstanding examples of Greek Revival, Georgian, and Federal architecture. Over the ensuing decades, "town and gown" have coexisted in peace and harmony that's only seriously disrupted when 80,000

UGA "Bulldog" football fanatics shake the skies over Sanford Stadium with exhortations of "Go-ooo Dawgs!"

Start your visit at the Athens Welcome Center, in the **Church-Waddel-Brumby House,** 280 East Dougherty Street, (706) 353–1820. The fine Federalist house was built in 1820 for Alonzo Church, who later became UGA's president. It's believed to be the city's oldest surviving residence. You may tour the lovely rooms and pick up information about other attractions and tours. It's open Tuesday through Saturday 10:00 A.M. to 5:00 P.M. and Sunday 2:00 to 5:00 P.M.

Classic City Tours (706–208–TOUR), led by Athens Convention and Visitors Bureau guides, take you through antebellum homes, gardens, and attractions around the city and university campus. You may also pick up a walking-driving tour map at the Welcome Center and see Athens at your own pace.

The **Taylor-Grady House,** 634 Prince Avenue, (706) 549–8688, was built in 1845. The thirteen Doric columns surrounding three sides of the Greek Revival showplace allegedly represent the original thirteen colonies, bound in a Union, just as the columns were bound by a wrought-iron railing. Now owned by the city of Athens, the rooms are filled with period antiques and open to the public Tuesday through Friday 10:00 A.M. to 3:30 P.M. Admission is $2.50.

Other classical residences that may be viewed from the outside include the University of Georgia president's home, a regal Greek Revival with fourteen Corinthian columns on the front and sides, and a parade of Doric columns facing a five-acre garden at the rear. It's in elite company at 570 Prince Avenue.

Civil War buffs shouldn't miss the **"Double-Barreled Cannon,"** a whimsical piece of memorabilia that was a spectacular failure. Cast in Athens in 1862, each barrel was to be loaded with cannonballs connected to each other by an 8-foot chain. When fired, the missiles were *supposed* to exit together, pull the chain tight, and sweep across the battlefield like a scythe. In reality, the barrels weren't synchronized, and instead of devastating Yankees, the errant shots plowed up a field, knocked down trees, and killed a cow. The beloved curiosity stands beside City Hall—pointing north, "just in case." **"The Tree That Owns Itself"** is another one-of-a-kind landmark. The 50-foot oak, at Dearing and Findley Streets, was granted its autonomy and 8 feet of land on all sides by a UGA professor many years ago.

The UGA campus is a treasury of classical and contemporary architecture. According to tradition freshmen are forbidden to walk through the University Arch, which dates to 1857 and leads to the stately old trees and venerable buildings of historic **North Campus.** Listed on the National Register of Historic Places, "Old North's" dowagers include Phi Kappa Hall, an 1836 Greek Revival; Federal-style Waddel Hall, 1820; Palladian-style Demosthenian Hall, 1824; Greek Revival University Chapel, whose bells joyously proclaim "Bulldog" football triumphs; and Old College, where in 1832 Crawford W. Long, a Georgian who'd later discover the use of anesthesia for surgery, roomed with Alexander Hamilton Stephens, who became vice-president of the Confederacy.

Elsewhere on the huge, sprawling campus, the permanent collections of the **Georgia Museum of Art** include more than 7,000 paintings, drawings, and sculptures by nineteenth- and twentieth-century American and European artists. Many important traveling exhibitions also stop here. The galleries are open daily, free of charge.

Flower and garden lovers should allot plenty of time for the **State Botanical Garden.** The 313-acre preserve of gardens, nature trails, a visitors center, and state-of-the-art conservatory contains thousands of native and exotic plants, large stands of trees, and small populations of white-tailed deer, raccoons, rabbits, and many species of birds. The visitors center/conservatory is open Monday through Saturday 9:00 A.M. to 4:30 P.M. and Sunday 11:30 A.M. to 4:30 P.M. The outdoor gardens and nature trails are open daily 8:00 A.M. to dusk. Lunch is served daily in the **Garden Cafe,** 2450 South Milledge Avenue, (706) 542–1244.

With all these thousands of perpetually ravenous students, finding a place to eat is no problem. For food-on-the-run, try the chili dogs, burgers, fries, sandwiches, and ice cream at the **Varsity,** 1000 West Broad Street, (706) 548–7160.

Restaurants, casual cafes, coffeehouses, and snack bars line Broad Street across from the UGA campus and spill onto adjacent streets. **Harry Bissett's New Orleans Cafe and Oyster Bar,** 237 East Broad across from the University Arch, (706) 353–7065, is a mainstay in a constantly shifting dining and entertainment scene. **Athens Brewing Company,** 312 East Washington Street, (706) 549–0027, is the city's first microbrew pub. **East/West Bistro,** 351 East Broad Street, (706) 546–9378, has a split casual/dress up–upstairs/downstairs personality where adventurous students and townies can get everything from three-cheese blintzes to chicken with pine nuts in phyllo pastry. Other wise just follow your nose and ask a friendly Bulldog for his or her recommendations.

Ditto when it comes to music. Athens is a spawning ground for modern rock bands. **The 40 Watt Club,** 285 West Washington Street, (706) 549–7879, still thrives on its reputation as the launching pad for REM and the B-52s back in the seventies. Local bands and touring groups also play the turn-of-the-century **Morton Theater** at 199 West Washington Street. Once the state's most famous Black vaudeville theater, the Morton has recently been restored to its former glory.

Bed-and-breakfast inns are perfect complements to Athens' antebellum landmarks. The **Old Winterville Inn,** in a quiet village 3 miles off Highway 78/Lexington Road, 7 miles east of Athens, dates back to the 1870s when it thrived as a traveling salesmen's hotel. Current owners Don and Julie Bower have restored the original board-and-batten clapboard exterior and the interior heart pine floors and hand-planed plank walls. Guest rooms have a bedroom, sitting room, kitchen, and private entrance and are $55 a double. It's at 108 South Main Street, Winterville 30683, (706) 742–7340. Book in advance if you're coming in June for Winterville's annual **Marigold Festival.**

Magnolia Terrace Guest House, 277 Hill Street, Athens 30601, (706) 548–3860 and (800) 891–1912, is in the historic district, near downtown and the university. Built in 1912, the handsome Colonial Revival mansion is rich with architectual treasures. Innkeeper Shelia Hackney's eight guest rooms have claw-foot tubs and modern showers. Guests can enjoy their continental breakfast in the dining room or on the wide front porch. Children and pets are welcome. Doubles are about $85.

Oconee County, Athens's southern neighbor, is the home of more than four dozen working craftspeople. Stop by the ◈ **Oconee County Welcome Center** in the small county seat of Watkinsville and pick up a *Guide to the Arts,* which will direct you to painters, potters, paper makers, weavers, metal smithies, iron forgers, jewelry crafters, broom and doll makers, and other artisans in Watkinsville and other small communities. Also free at the welcome center, *A Walking Tour of Main Street Watkinsville* describes fifty homes, churches, shops, and public buildings in Victorian, Greek Revival, Plantation Plain, Gothic, Federal, and other styles. The welcome center is housed in the historic **Eagle Tavern.** In the late 1700s and early 1800s, the Eagle's bar and beds made it a welcome stop on the Charleston–New Orleans stagecoach route.

In case you believe New England has a monopoly on covered bridges, ◆ **Watson Mill Bridge State Park** will be a pleasant surprise. Off Highway 22 east of Athens, the 144-acre park is the site of Georgia's longest covered bridge. Four spans of the century-old wooden bridge stretch 236 feet across the South Fork of the Broad River. It's an idyllic spot for a picnic, canoeing, and an overnight stay in the campground. For reservations phone (800) 864–PARK, or contact Park Superintendent, Route 1, Comer 30629, (706) 783–5349.

Athens is the northern anchor of "The Antebellum Trail," an association of historic towns along Highway 441 in east-central Georgia. For further information on Athens, contact the Convention and Visitors Bureau, P.O. Box 948, Athens 30603, (706) 546–1805.

INDEXES

Entries for Festivals and Folk Plays, Museums, National Parks and Historic Sites, and State Parks and Historic Sites appear in the special indexes on pages 164-66.

162

Special Indexes

Festivals and Folk Plays

Museums

National Parks and Historic Sites

State Parks and Historic Sites

About the Author

William Schemmel is a full-time freelance writer and photographer who travels from Paris, Texas, to Paris, France, but most enjoys telling others about his native state of Georgia. His work appears regularly in numerous magazines, newspapers, and guidebooks. A member of the Society of American Travel Writers, he has experienced adventures on Georgia's off-the-beaten-paths for more than twenty-five years. He invites you to get off the interstate highways and make your own fascinating discoveries.